ACROSS THE GREEN

Edward Roberts

Edited by John G Bygate

*The History of Education Project wishes to express its most grateful thanks
to the family of Edward Roberts
and to the Durham branch of the National Union of Mineworkers
for their support in the production of this volume*

part of
THE HISTORY OF EDUCATION PROJECT
Miners Hall, Red Hill, Durham DH1 4BB
(tel/fax: 0191 370 9941)

CONTENTS

ᎶᏋᏐᎧ

ILLUSTRATIONS

(following p.44)

All the above illustrations come from the Roberts family archives with the exception of no.3, for which thanks are due to Doreen Cowan.

The drawing on the front cover (and in part on the title page) is by Norman Cornish (©) and reproduced by permission of the University Art Gallery, University of Northumbria, Newcastle-upon-Tyne

INTRODUCTION

This is an exceptional story of an exceptional member of a North-East mining family whose parents, remarkably, managed to send him to training college before the First World War.

It is a social documentary of life in a Durham mining community in the early part of the twentieth century, described on an intimate level to show the impact of events on children and schools written by one who was himself pupil, student, teacher, headmaster and finally inspector of schools. (It can rightly be said that his school days only ended with retirement.) The hard life of early schools, methods of teaching, hardships in learning and the harsh exercise of authority are vividly described. So too are the glimpses of boyhood in a miner's home and at the local Baptist chapel, so often a powerhouse of family (and local) activities.

The Project is indebted to the family of Edward Roberts (1893-1974) for its cooperation in the production of this book. His two daughters, Julie Mar and Kathleen Hogarth, are very pleased that, after all the time and effort spent by their father in writing his memoirs, the first part, covering his younger days, has at least and at last been set in print. They wish to acknowledge the help and encouragement of two other members of the Roberts family, Enid Welch and Freda Barker, and of Tom Mar and Joyce Mitchell, who provided the initial inspiration to get this work into print.

The memoirs have been carefully edited by John Bygate.

G R Batho
(Emeritus Professor of Education)
March 2003

Mount Pleasant c.1900 (based on 1896 OS map)

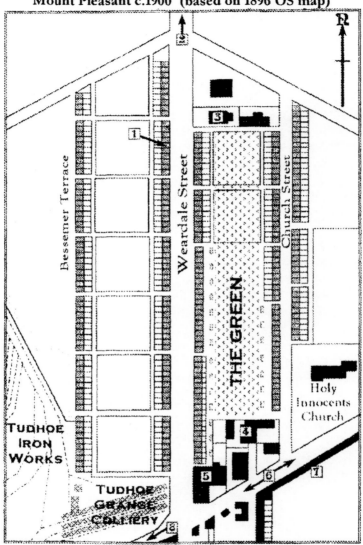

1 – 30 Weardale Street, where the Roberts family first lived
2 – Tudhoe Village   3 – Presbyterian church
4 – Mount Pleasant Junior School   5 – Methodist chapel
6 – Half Moon Lane   7 – the music shop
8 – Merrington Lane, "Chuckie's" pond and the "sleeper wall"

THE GREEN

The Green in Mount Pleasant had never been known by any other name. In dark and in light, in summer and in winter, people always spoke of The Green, yet within living memory it had never been green. It was clay, a horrible yellowish-brown clay.

Once upon a time green grass did grow on that spot. In early summer, when the gorse blazed, the scene was pleasant to the eye. But gold and green disappeared when, searching for coal, men dug deep into the earth and piled their dross on its surface.

Then homes were built there for the men who would dig and hew the coal. Let it be said that the coal-owners did not plan or create a slum. Instead, they gave men room to live. Over the open countryside, where sheep and cattle had grazed, long terraces of clean stone houses rose, running north to south, broken into convenient blocks of ten or twenty: Church Street, Weardale Street, Bessemer Terrace — proud names. The place had character. The houses of Weardale Street faced each other across a generous space containing a wide road neatly defined by a broad grass verge on either side. For a mining area this was indeed distinction.

The backs of the houses, though, were less attractive, their rough stone contrasting with the smooth, dressed surface at the front. Yet at the rear of the row on the eastern side of Weardale Street - to the great surprise of all who came upon it - there stretched the long, wide rectangular space called The Green. In days when 'planning' was rare and 'development' known only on specially selected sites, this broad, open space was preserved for men whose days were spent in sunless under-ground tunnels, to be used by them for recreation and by their children to romp and play on. With imagination unleashed it might have become a very pleasant place, a model mining estate. But this was no time for aesthetic indulgence. There was coal to win and homes to be built. The men themselves could use the space as they wished.

At the Green's northern end a Presbyterian church gave shelter from the winter wind, and men and women exiled from the beloved place of their birth sang within its walls the psalms that gave shelter from other winds that chilled their lives. At the northern end too wise men fenced off land for gardens and saved the soil. Encroachment then took place at the margins, where were built crees and pens to house poultry and pigs - structures of such wood as a man might beg, borrow or steal; of no regular pattern; frequently crudely original in design; nearly always ugly; and finally rendered totally repulsive with a coat of tar that sealed the crevices as the huge brush satisfyingly spread the thick liquid on every side. Men admired their own handiwork, but it did not improve the landscape - far from it.

On the open south side the level line of magnesium limestone swung away north-east to the sea. At the foot of the scarp undulated a wide expanse of gorse and broom, a sea of golden fire in the summer that thrilled the eye of those who strolled across the green or wheeled their babies in the sun. When, however, they built the schools across this southern gap, men exchanged sight of burning bush for a high, windowless wall of stone.

So the Green was enclosed. Without any society for the preservation of green and pleasant places, with no exercise of authority - public or private - to save it from destruction, The Green became brown, and bare earth showed its ugly, ochrous face.

The periphery of the Green served as drying-ground for the weekly washday. On lines slung between tall posts fixed deep into the earth there flapped in the wind garments familiar and less familiar, in blacks and greys, navy-blues and browns, vivid reds and whites - but mostly in sober colours that saved on washing and that could be worn any time. Most houses had their own posts; a few shared with neighbours. To night-time wanderers their irregular spacing made them a menace; in daylight they were an offence to the eye. Moreover, these long lateral flanks were decorated at intervals with blocks of "netties", the only form of toilets provided in those days, which necessitated a long, arduous walk from the house, especially in bad weather.

What might have been a pleasant place frayed at the edges. Decay spread inwards, the grass perished, and the place thereof knew it no more.

But everyone still spoke of The Green.

C3ຂວ

6

THE FOLK

My father was a coalminer, whose family came from North Wales. His parents had moved when the pits in the North-east offered more attractive prospects. To cover the distance on foot, their belongings in a bundle on a stick, was itself achievement. A few of their fellows had enough money to travel part of the way by coach, train or cart, perhaps, but they often had to complete the journey on foot. In the 1860s and 1870s the trickle became a stream. Beyond the Midlands they mingled with folk from Staffordshire and Derbyshire. The migrants often became little communities long before they reached the places where the new pits had been sunk. Fifty years later the dialects they had refused to surrender still baffled us.

The Welsh remained consciously a separate section of the community wherever they settled. Here they founded three chapels, on separate theological differences that were so characteristic of the nineteenth century. Among these folk the bond of nationality was stronger even than their theological conviction, and when they were caught up in singing only one thing mattered — their native land, with its songs from the heart to move even the dullest of souls. They were almost all identified by such names as Jones, Morris, Owens, Roberts, Griffiths, Hughes, Lloyd, Thomas, Evans and Williams, but their attempts to distinguish between family members by the use of Christian names — for example, David John Jones and John David Jones — did little to help.

My mother's family was from Staffordshire. Among the folk from Derbyshire and Staffordshire there was no such unifying influence. Scattered throughout the community they were more frequently separate individuals. Some of the best - strong personalities, highly intelligent and with high ideals - identified themselves with the Primitive Methodist movement, where their singing, sermons and prayers were without the restraint that characterized the worship of other sects.

But certain others gave them no cause for pride in their origin.

These were the fellows who might be pointed out as "terrible in drink". When the fortnightly 'pay Friday' came round, this less responsible section visited the pubs before their wives could get hold of their money. Such a figure would come home at night with little or nothing in his pockets and belly and head swollen with drink. He would storm in and clear the house as if a cyclone had struck, the family fleeing into the street. Then the sodden creature would appear in the yard, loudly cursing all and sundry. His shouts brought out the neighbours - but folk kept their distance; any who dared approach were threatened with the breadknife he had grabbed from the kitchen. Quiet returned only when he fell exhausted onto the cold bricks of the yard. In concern and disgust the family carried him in to sleep it off on a hard couch. Next morning the roaring lion walked the street again, sheepish and sullen, avoided by decent folk. A fortnight later the scene would be re-enacted. They always said he would kill someone before he was finished ... but usually the drink killed him first.

The Irish had come to work at the Iron and Steel Works (though some were navvies) and tended to live in one overcrowded quarter, much inferior to the areas where the miners dwelt. This was where the strongest addiction to nationality was to be found. Moreover, their streets contained more public houses than any other part of Spennymoor. The scorching heat of the furnaces made men thirsty, and if they turned into the pubs at eight o'clock instead of going home for breakfast, it was because they thought there was more nourishment in beer than in bacon - and it was easier to put it 'on the slate'.

The steelworkers earned big money and they were big spenders ... but without appearing to be the better off for it. The pubs beckoned invitingly, and nightly a crowd forgot the day's work and consumed the week's brass at The Ironworks Hotel, The Vulcan Hotel, The Puddlers' Arms, The Foundry Inn and The Steam Mill Inn. Those who liked contemplation and quiet talk over a pint preferred The Victoria, The Golden Fleece and Hearts of Oak. We were well served with churches, chapels and, above all, pubs.

Saturday night was celebration night. The cares of the week were over, spirits ran high and new energy abounded. They showed how much each could take, these men of iron. Some took too much. Hard drinking led to hard blows in the bar, after which they would be thrown out onto the street, where, stripping themselves of jacket and shirt, they hammered each other with bare fists, until such a noisy scene developed that men from inside came running out to separate the often blood-spattered pair, or the sight of a policeman caused wholesale flight round the back streets. By the time the law actually arrived, however, there was not a soul in sight. (We small boys used to anticipate these riotous occasions, and played opposite the pubs in readiness for what should follow. But when the 'bobby' was sighted, we too took to our heels and spent the rest of the summer evening playing on the Green in safety).

There was more than a sprinkling of Scots. For hundreds of years they had savagely invaded the North, but these invaders came in peace, in order to work. They were good, upright folk, their lilting speech a joy to the ear (though sometimes unintelligible), and in their deeds they were honourable and honest, befitting the Presbyterianism of which they were so proud and which they believed set them above all other men such as Irish and Welsh and Midlanders ... yet *just* a little lower than the angels, perhaps. They regarded themselves as highly respectable ornaments of society, worshipping God with a dignity and reverence that contrasted greatly with the ranting style used by the more evangelical sections of Nonconformity, which made them shudder.

It was among the mining community, regardless of county or country of origin, that the strongest ties developed. These folk shared all the dangers of the dark underground, with injury and death ever present, as well as suffering and shortage. They worked together as "marras" (or mates) at the coalface, even sharing their earnings; together they made a living by reason of sheer physical strength. In this way they acquired a tremendous strength of character that expressed itself in the valiant struggle against the common enemy, whoever or whatever that might be, and in a matchless loyalty to their fellows and to all good causes. They were men without education but with standards of fairness that would shame more enlightened folk in the wider community. They were bluntly outspoken, meaning what they said - yet beneath the tough skin (blue-streaked with coal dust on hand or head) there was a touching tenderness. Their kids were 'the bairns', and that can only be said tenderly. They were folk who were friends for life.

To enter a miner's kitchen was to share a warmth and friendliness as real as the huge, brightly burning fire in the hearth that dominated one side of the room, the shining brasses lighting up the mantelpiece and the most shining steel fender that ever woman gave herself to. The smell of metal polish and bath-brick on Fridays was something to avoid, but the women loved it.

The steel fender was an imposing decoration for the hearth. About five feet long, extending the length of the hearth, sometimes nearly a foot high, and as broad, rounded at the ends, its flat upper surface pleasingly designed, it prevented too close contact with the fire. In an emergency or for a comfortable seat either end was ample enough to support even the bulkiest. There, with hands clasped round the knees, one leaned gently forward and in that comfortable posture gossip flowed freely or meditation ran deep. But it was on baking day that the fender and the hearth had their finest hour. To buy bread was undreamed of. The best qualifications the would-be miner's wife could possess were the ability to bake bread, satisfying home-made bread, and to cook a substantial meal.

In a huge earthenware dish mother would mix her flour, salt, yeast and water, knead it patiently and thoroughly, then set the dish before the hearth for the dough to rise. When it was ready, it was kneaded again, then pieces were cut off and placed into loaf tins, lightly greased. These were set again along the fender and on the hearth for a while and then put into the oven to bake. With the fire stoked up to full heat, the whole room became a furnace, while the woman walked the floor, enduring the heat as a matter of pride. Prouder still they were when the smell of those lovely, golden-brown, freshly-baked loaves filled the house and confirmed their skill in the baker's craft. Twelve beautifully-shaped loaves cooling on the table, with teacakes alongside. Here was consummate artistry in homecraft. Little wonder that these folk despised the bought loaf. On homemade bread with butter carefully, thinly spread one could make a satisfying meal.

And sometimes that was all there was. Some did not always have butter - only a layer of beef dripping, maybe, saved from the weekend roast beef joint - sometimes given a tasty variation by a sprinkling of salt and pepper - or a thin, very thin, spread of jam. But the connoisseur, and I counted myself one, loved the fresh, crunchy crust from the end of a newly-baked loaf. It was some-thing to get one's teeth into and to chew for its soft sweetness. But times have changed. The fender has gone from most homes - it took too much cleaning. And homemade bread, too, has almost gone, like the unhasty age of our youth. Baking day was an all-absorbing operation. Why toil and sweat? It's as cheap to buy it nowadays

CBEO

THE FAMILY

My parents became an integral part of this mixed society, whose men toiled together and whose women lived together, borrowing a loaf when they ran out of bread and repaying on baking day, sharing the open space of the Green with their lines on washing days, their children scrapping together in the street, on the Green and in the school play-ground. In this crazy blend were to be found all the elements of a stable society. And the first creature my eyes looked upon when I came into the world was the breezy, blue—eyed Scotswoman who acted as midwife, uncertificated and untrained except through the regular practice of officiating at births in miners' homes, where a large family was the norm. She herself had only one child. Her affection was showered on us.

I never knew my father's parents. His father was 'Taid' (pronounced "tide") - the Welsh word for father. He died several years before I was born and I was named after him. Grandmother was 'Nain' (pronounced "nine") to us and she came to live with our young family. I can see her still, her slight figure dressed always in black, the long skirt trailing the floor, a black woollen shawl over her narrow shoulders. She busied herself quietly, seen but not heard. One wintry day in February she passed away, and though I was only a small boy I was sent across the Green to Aunt Lizzie's with the news. Two days earlier the succession of three boys had been broken by the birth of another girl, to be named Mary, after 'Nain'. So one life began and another ended. It has indeed been a gift of renewal.

I knew my maternal grandfather, 'old Joe', though only when I was a small boy, for he died in his early sixties, bowed, bent and broken. When he walked those two hundred miles from the old place in Staffordshire he must have bowed his head even then in the thoughtful silence that always seemed to envelop him. You always knew when he was thinking. He never hurried. Meditation and haste were incompatibles, but even when you had to wait and wait for him, it was worth it. Less opinionated than many of his fellows, he was tolerant and ready to listen, acknowledging there were few answers to the issues of life and death, unlike some folk endowed with a fiery certitude. It made things easier if one believed as straightforwardly as they did, but he felt it was not so simple. His greatest desire was to see books of philosophy, poetry and religion cheaper and more easily available. He knew he would never have other than this simple home and this frugal living, but when he left the house to meet the lads at the street corner or at the chapel class meeting, in mind and spirit he was an aristocrat.

Emma rubbed his chest. There was always goose-grease in the house, collected at Christmas-time wherever a lucky family could spare it. Emma had appeared in Joe's life when, while coming home once from work, he was rendered helpless in the street by a terrible fit of coughing. She took him in charge on the spot, and they soon married. A wizened little thing she was, but she washed, scrubbed, ironed, baked and cooked for him, as a woman ought, all tirelessly. She had a tongue as fierce as lightning, but to Joe she could be ever so tender. Then, for no apparent reason, it could suddenly shrill out to set your teeth on edge.

She could not follow him when he talked about the books he read, for she had never learned to read. She knew what he liked to eat, and he boasted of her dumplings and stews, and the cheap joints she found for the weekend. On Sunday evenings, in her black bonnet, black cloak and long skirt trailing the ground, she walked slowly to the chapel. Most of the hymns she knew by heart. The sermon was a distant background for the sucking and crushing of hard-boiled sweets, and a good measure of the length of the sermon was the number of sweets left in the packet.

She had her own problems though, in her two sons and three daughters. David, the elder son, was dignified in manner, gentle in speech and intellectual in taste and outlook, while his conversation revealed in the young man a quality of mind and depth of thought that his ranter father knew could well outstrip him.

Solomon, his brother, was as tall as David, though standing together he seemed six inches less. He never stood upright. His head drooped forward, his back was arched, and his shoulders sagged. His arms and legs seemed to collapse at the joints when he walked ... or shuffled, rather, and he never moved in a straight line. In his carriage he was neither upright nor direct, and when he approached, with his long shuffle, his body rising and falling with its hinged limbs and his brown eyes staring fixedly in front of him, men turned away in distrust. His was a mathematical mind but they did not trust his figures, and others learned not to trust his signature. Self—educated David went into coal, Solomon into iron and steel. They were born too early for their abilities to have real opportunity.

The girls too were greatly contrasted.

Caroline towered over all the family. Over six feet tall, with a framework of sharp-angled bones and taut muscles, she throbbed with rude pride as she looked down on the others. Her black hair was pulled tight over the head and screwed at the back. Tightly compressed lips showed a merciless face. Somewhere in the family's genealogical line there must have been a Red Indian squaw. She struck terror as she stood, baring her chiselled teeth through which men knew she spat fury when taunted. She lived in a perpetual state of war.

The dominating presence of Caroline led Phoebe and Rachel to withdraw whenever they could. Phoebe was nearly as tall as Caroline, almost as bony and angular but not as aggressive, with actually an endearing quality in her voice unexpected in one of her physique.

Rachel was the youngest. It seemed as if she had all the virtues and graces the others lacked: she was the smallest, the quietest, the most gently spoken — the one with a vision and a sense of lovely things. When the whole family sat at Sunday dinner, Rachel was the tender plant among this rough growth.

Old Joe thanked the Lord that his lot had fallen in this pleasant place, despite the thorns. His rocking chair by the fire was his comfort; there he swung gently to and fro, the big Bible on his knees and the long-stemmed clay pipe reaching from his mouth beyond the pages. He knew by heart the wanderings of Abraham and Moses and was as patriarchal as they had been, for his tribes were as much trouble as theirs. On the Sabbath, in a crowded Methodist chapel — to which he walked the seven miles, also returning on foot — miners, with all their bones still aching from their battles at the coalface, brought their wives, lads and lasses to see and hear Old Joe. There he stood — bent and bowed, with his white hair and yellow—white beard, his dreamy eyes beneath bushy eyebrows, afflicted with bronchitis from his years of work — as he led them through their wilderness of black sorrow to a land of shining light ... a land that Moses never knew. And later, as he walked away from them into the black night, mopping his streaming head with a huge red and white spotted handkerchief, they shouted many a blessing after him. They would have much to talk about next day as the cage took them down to the dark depths again.

At two o'clock next morning, when he rose to put on his clothes for work, Emma followed — faithful as ever — to give him his mug of tea and a bit of bread and dripping. He went quietly out into the chill of the early morning, listening over the sound of his heavy boots for the sound of his 'marras' as from different points they approached the street corner that was their rendezvous and shelter from the hard night.

These were men on whom their society was firmly and surely based. They shared all their lives, they shared their work and they shared the pay. In each other's home they talked as if there were but one home, shared the delights of each other's children; they were one family with one faith.

They were all there, so, silently, they moved off together, past the long rows where kith and kin lived, where a faint glow in the back rooms showed the fire recently re-kindled. Over the wasteland of The Green they went, where feet alone guided them through the pitch darkness across the uneven surface, past more rows of sleeping houses. Only then - on this Monday morning, before the lark sang and long before the cock crowed - did they begin to talk with a quiet exultation of yesterday at their chapels. Now they could face with renewed faith and hope another week of black toil and dark danger.

୧୫⬥୫ଦ

14

FAMILY LIFE

I was born early one Sunday morning in July 1893. The previous day had been the day of the year in Durham - Miners' Gala Day. I was just too late for that occasion, but in after years it gave me some of the greatest thrills a man could feel - and I was never a miner.

Speaking of my birth my parents would always say, "You were born the year after the Big Strike." The Big Strike! In the early summer of 1892 the mine-owners demanded a reduction of 13½ per cent on standard rates of pay; though the miners were prepared to make some con-cession, the owners were unyielding. For three months the men stood in the streets. Their funds were negligible. All that was available was ten shillings per member and five per half member. From outside sources no substantial help came. It took a thousand pounds to give every member four-pence! Most mining families were members of Co-operative Societies and so could draw on their dividend savings, but these were soon exhausted; with no organized means of support the people experienced acute distress. When finally Bishop Westcott brought the two sides together in his home in Auckland Castle, the miners agreed after a grim struggle to accept a reduction of ten per cent.

There could be no quick return to work, however, so some remained unemployed for months; yet in the darkest hours of this trial, their endurance and self-control never wavered. They had been beaten, but not broken. They would rise again.

* * * * *

Payday for miners was once a fortnight. We early learned to distinguish Pay Friday and 'Baff' Friday, and the family budget over a fortnight called for the highest skill on the part of the housewife.

In a way we were fortunate. Father usually arranged with his 'marras' that he should be in fore shift, going out in the very early hours of the morning and returning about eleven. After dinner and a

15

bath by the fire he spent the afternoon in bed. After tea he gave lessons on the organ and the piano and so supplemented the meagre pay of a miner.

Mother was a useful needlewoman; assisted by three or four young women who came to her as apprentices, she was kept fully occupied in making articles of dress to order. How she managed is a cause for wonder, for at intervals of two years there came an addition to the family. But we all thrived, and every day when we came home from school a hot dinner was ready for us. No fancy dishes, but always plain, good food, and never anything left. We learned to clean our plates but we were never hungry. In the severe cold of the winter there were pans of delicious broth, thick with barley and all kinds of vegetables and rich with the flavour of ham bones. Lovely dumplings, too, and, if we were lucky, there were bits of ham and slices of bread. There was always plenty to fill the corners.

A miner's pay varied greatly according to his place in the pit. Some places were good, where coal was easily worked; some were hard, with thin seams and often much water. The places were drawn by ballot each quarter on a day called "cavilling" (or kevilling) day". For everyone it was a day of anxiety. After months of hard slogging with little to take home they would hope that at long last, their luck would change. There was no minimum wage then, and if a man and his 'marra' could not make sufficient to live on, they depended entirely on the goodwill of the manager to add to it. So the 'cavil' was a matter of luck, as was life. When they were lucky they lived well. When they were unlucky, life was hard. Life was a gamble, so many gambled and gambled hard, on anything and everything.

But we children were spared these worries, and each week we were given our 'pay penny'. So precious was this that the first thing to be done was to change it for two ha'pennies, to be spent one at a time, and we made sure we got value for money.

Yet life was precarious for the miner in more ways than one. As I returned from school one afternoon, the empty kitchen drew me to seek mother in the front room. She was standing at the front door, gazing at a house a few doors away. I squeezed past her. There in the street stood a jumbled heap of furniture, pots and pans, pictures, clothing, everything that had hitherto found its place in that home.

When I asked what was going on, she replied simply, "It's Bill Griffiths; he's been turned out." I was very young, but old enough to understand. Bill Griffiths was a Union man, vigorously promoting the cause of miners in the Union they had formed. The manager had warned him, but Bill persisted, his defiance had cost him his job and even his house. Having failed to oblige by removing from the house, he and his family were being forcibly evicted. With nowhere to go they stood dejectedly in the street. Before dark, however, all their belongings were transferred to a room in the church at the top of the street, and through the kindness of the elders the family were allowed to stay there till they found somewhere else to live.

So at a very early age I learned what it cost men to fight for causes in which they believed with passionate zeal. Through such sacrificial struggles was the Union established.

In the still, dark hours of the night we were sometimes roused from sleep by loud, resounding blows on the back door. This was the 'caller' on one of his nightly rounds. Beside each door the miner chalked on the wall the hour at which he was to be knocked up, and at the appropriate time the 'caller' came. No one could sleep through his summons - more to hell than heaven - and from the inside of the house boomed back a sound that showed the sleeper had wakened. We would hear father descend the stairs and stir the fire, and we knew that, after a cup of tea, he would slip his bait tin, filled the night before, and his tin bottle into his jacket pockets and walk out into the darkness to begin a new day.

We had fallen into our second sleep one night, and father was still moving about below, when the silence of the night was shattered by the long, piercing scream of a woman. Nothing of horror or agony or terror had come to us like that before. We were terrified in our bed. We heard father go out into the street and mother hurrying downstairs and outside. They were away some time. Through the bedroom window we could see the black shape of a van and a horse, and some men standing around. From within a house came the cries and sobs of a woman, and we could see other women, neighbours called from their beds, entering the house.

That was how death came to our street. Without warning the poor woman had been confronted at the back door in the middle of the night with the ambulance containing the body of her husband killed on the night shift by a fall of stone. With such primitive lack of ceremony were the dead brought home.

We lay awake till mother came in. She told us about Mick's father. Poor Mick, I thought. We played together a lot, and now he had no dad. I wondered if my father would always come back safely.

A gambler's life. Gambling with death - every day and every night. No wonder these folk shared their losses and found an indestructible strength in their common life.

* * * * *

On Sunday evenings my parents used to go to service. Father was choirmaster and organist. We children were left in the care of one of our older sisters. If we were good, we were told, she could make us some toffee, and sugar and butter and other ingredients were carefully measured out for that most likely eventuality and left in the pantry.

But there was one fly in the ointment ... brother Tom. He was two years younger than I and already had a reputation for defying authority. How would he behave? As father was about to leave the room, he turned round and, fixing his gaze on the small seven-year-old figure, he called in the severest tone, "Now Tom, remember". Then turning to the sister in charge - Ada on this occasion - he added, "If he starts any trouble, knock through for Mrs. Drake." (Mrs. Drake lived next door and knew the signal. Sharp, repeated knocking on the wall meant, "Come at once".)

We began very well indeed. We held our own little service, opening with a hymn, then the Lord's Prayer and another hymn, after which we recited the Twenty-third Psalm (the one we knew best), followed by another hymn (our repertoire was wide), but, as no-one could preach a sermon, the service had to come to an end at that point. What to do next?

It was then that the trouble began. One of us wanted to read a story, another to have turns in the rocking chair, another to play pirates on the sofa. But whatever was finally agreed on, Tom refused to accept majority rule and reacted so devastatingly that life was imperilled – or so we thought. Persuasion failing, there remained our last hope. It was Ada's decision to knock on the wall ...

That should have frightened him - but it did not. Round and round the room he surged, while we looked towards the door, listened for the lifting of the latch, dodging his blows or closing with him.

At last in came Mrs. Drake. Short but well-built and strong, wearing spectacles that seemed a little small for her broad face, she looked through them as if she could rule a kingdom. In one hand she held a tall horsewhip upright like a lance by her side, the handle resting on the floor. It towered above her head, the long tapering thong curving down to the floor. Why she kept it we never knew, but it could and did bring calm to our troubled seas when father was out.

Silence fell. Tom had retired from the fray and curled up in the rocking-chair, but she knew the cause of the trouble.

"Do you want a taste of this?" she asked him.

"No," he obliged, hesitant but still truculent.

"Then settle yourself down or you *will* get a taste of it, and more when your father comes in."

At last she withdrew. We looked at each other wistfully - little Wilf, Mary and I. These things would happen, but nothing had been broken. That was a very good thing.

What should we do now?

Ada solved our problem. "Shall I make the toffee?" It seemed that it did not quite fit the rules, but we all thought it would be a lovely thing to do - just the right thing - and she brought out the pan, the butter and the sugar. Before long we were gazing at the brown liquid simmering gently in the pan, watching it being poured into the tin and placed in the pantry to cool. And while it was cooling, with finger and spoon we cleaned out the inside of the pan as thoroughly as ever kitten licked its saucer clean.

No toffee tasted like that delicious, homemade, Sabbath-breaking toffee. There was even some left to wrap and take to school next morning for playtime. Going to bed after that was quite a pleasure.

C3ED

"ON CHRISTMAS  NIGHT ..."

It was on Christmas Eve that we children were introduced to the joys of the family party, though only in a limited way at first. Quite early in the evening we smaller children were bathed and made ready for bed so as to be out of the way before our Welsh uncle and aunt and cousins arrived for supper.

Before going upstairs, however, a very important ceremonial had to be observed. For each of us a pair of clean black or grey long woollen stockings was taken from a drawer. Each pair was secured at the top by a large safety pin that also held a small piece of paper bearing our names - Edward, Tom, Wilf, Mary, Beatrice and Gladys. They were slung over the brass rail that ran under the mantelpiece and left there to await the arrival of Santa Claus. With a last injunction to mother that she must be sure to tell Santa what we wanted, we were ushered up the stairs by Maggie, while Lily and Ada continued to help mother with the supper.

While we slept, the relatives arrived. As supper was eaten with loud delight and uproarious explosions of laughter at the recollection of happy years, the noise gradually broke our sleep.

"Can we come down now?" we called.

Conversation stilled; consultation was taking place. Then at last Lily called to us, "Yes, you may come down now."

Down we trundled, blinking as we entered the lighted, smoke-filled room, to an outburst of amused and sympathetic comments from all.

We stole a look at the stockings on the line and we looked at each other in sad surprise. They were still empty.

"Santa hasn't been yet," cried aunt, seeing our surprise. "He won't come till you have gone back to bed."

There was complete agreement. We looked around bewildered.

"Come on my knee," called first one and then another, and soon we were all seated, myself on the fender beside Lily.

"Now be careful there, don't sit too near the fire. We don't want Christmas spoilt for everybody." And so in gentle banter and fond indulgence we were made to feel so happy.

Then the singing began. My uncle's family were nearly all grown up, several were married, and all were present, husbands and wives. With all of us there - brothers and sisters, father and mother - the choir was complete, a real four-part choir.

"Come on, Thomas." said John to Father, "Start us off", and from the first note they were away together, as always. Father was conductor of the chapel choir, and all knew the importance of good attack. Fired with Celtic fervour they overcame the handicap of a heavy supper and lifted their heads. Their singing held us children spellbound, though at times we were nigh on deafened by it! We soon picked up the parts and enjoyed ourselves as much as our elders. The room, though, should have been three times the size for that exuberant singing.

The origin of the song we never knew. It was a family song, sung as long as we remember and by no one else. The words sound trite, but for joy of singing this was a Christmas treat. With what abandon they pealed the big bells and jingled the sleigh bells. Uncle John raised his arms as if holding the rope and to the rhythm of the opening bar of the chorus, with its mighty JING, JING, pulled so mightily that he nearly sent cups and saucers flying from the table. Towards the last two lines the song moved with gradually quickening tempo till jing-jing-jing-jing became merely a chain of sound that swept to a triumphant end.

A dramatic, spellbinding silence followed, while we wondered what would happen next. Then Uncle John boomed out in his deep bass, "Once again, ring the bells," and they sang it anew. Only grudgingly did they stop. They could have gone on forever, but they must pause for breath sometimes. Then they laughed as loudly as they had sung.

After a while they knew what to do. "Let's have a quiet one now." Everyone knew which it would be — "Silent Night". The quiet beauty of its gently lilting melody floated across the room. There was no place for piano or organ in this room, but the singing was better without it, for then you heard the voices. The words were here and there unsure, but no-one stopped singing; it was music without words. Here, as on the poetic night when the Babe was born, angels sang. Something so deep in our joy found its most wonderful expression in song. Two families under one roof in a miner's home. The memory is ineffaceable.

"Silent Night," had to be our lullaby. It was a convenient point for mother to whisper, "You had better go back up now. Santa won't call here if he knows you are not in bed."

Disregarding the fear of bad dreams through late eating, Auntie said we should have something from the table before we left. "Give them a mince pie," she urged, and a plate was passed across. The pies looked too good to eat, even though they were now only slightly warm, yet they deserved the short shrift we gave them. And then, amidst a chorus of "Good-night," and "Merry Christmas", we climbed the stairs again.

"Wasn't it lovely?" we all said as we scrambled into bed.

It had been like a story come to life to go downstairs in the middle of the night and see everyone so genuinely happy.

Such moments were rare treats ... for grown-ups and children alike.

CB∞

THE OTHER SIDE OF THE GREEN

The Green was a broad highway. No road was marked, no path defined. You crossed it anywhere, this no man's land, this common land. Coalman, butcher and milkman, greengrocer and lamp-oil vendors all chose their own way, their carts slowly dipping and rising on the broken surface like ships on the ocean. The horses knew the undulations as well as their drivers. We, too, charted our path to school, looking with concern at our shiny boots (freshly blacked each night) and hoping against hope that their polished uppers would be preserved from pool and puddle for our entry into school.

School! Its wall rose grim and austere as if hiding fearful secrets. A solid timber gate ten feet high, suspended from iron runners, marked the limit of freedom. To look at it was to be warned not to enter. When you walked out through that door, you felt you had escaped. Behind that forbidding wall the Church sought to kindle the light of learning and the knowledge of eternal truth: it might at least have made entrance more attractive.

I was three years old when I crossed the Green to start school. Before the morning was half spent, I was missing the quiet of home and the care of my mother. I cried; I would not be comforted. When the Headmistress and her assistant failed to restore my spirits, my eldest sister was sent for from 'the big school'. She was nine and had already learned to mother two sisters. With her I was at ease again, and the rocking-horse, solitary plaything of the baby-room, became a newfound joy. After that the new environment was acceptable.

We were soon plunged into learning. The alphabet and its mysteries were the royal road along which we travelled to the singing delights of phonic reading. Huge charts were slung over the blackboard and to the rhythm of the teacher's pitch-pine pointer we chanted lustily: *c-an, can; f-an, fan; p-an, pan; r-an, ran.*

From the single word, laden with symbolism, we passed to the story. *Dan has a can.......Dan has a pan.......Dan has a can and a pan.*

23

Who Dan was we never knew, and what kind of person he was to have a can and a pan was a mystery that was not ours to solve. We were learning to read. What sense the reading made did not matter, and when at a later stage we could read 'Lo an ox is by me so', the heights of fantastic nonsense were scaled.

And yet ... we learned to read: Teacher saw to that. It was the most important part of the day and occupied most of it, though some time was allotted to sums. It was then I discovered the chief use for fingers was to count on; so indispensable were they for this that, long after we had left the Infants, many boys continued to use their fingers - sometimes openly, sometimes under the desk - without disapproval.

It was in this lesson too that the heavens opened. The noise reached out beyond the playground to the Green. Beginning slowly and quietly - twice one are two; twice two are four - the rhythm gradually quickened, and the sound grew. Twice three are six; twice four are eight; twice five are TEN . Now the rhythm was speeding up, the volume increasing.

Beyond this point some uncertainty began to show itself in the muted hesitance about the final number in each line, but the shrill challenge of the Amazon teacher fanning the blaze with her "Shout up, now!" was the signal to those of us who thought we knew the answers to fill our lungs and swell the chorus, while those less sure watched our lips and followed, a fraction of a second later, correctly but meaninglessly: Twice nine are EIGHTEEN, Twice ten are TWENTY. As we reached TWICE TWELVE ARE TWENTY-FOUR, our cries were of pure ecstasy. But that was the end; in triumph we collapsed.

Yet how many twenty-four were, I did not know; I had never had twenty-four of anything. Yet that was what the 'song' said: TWICE TWELVE ARE TWENTY-FOUR. Ah, yes ... then I remembered ... four and twenty blackbirds baked in a pie! That was it! Twice twelve ... baked in a pie. It was good enough for me - as true as the engraved tablets of stone that Moses had so laboriously carried down the mountain and dropped.

Simultaneous chanting - no need for breathing exercises! Our tables did that for us. To vary the monotony of this feverish, deafening chant we would cup our hands over our ears, press hard to shut out the noise, then release to taste the din; cup them again and release, in a rhythm of our own, which we varied from time to time. We had discovered a playway to learning all on our own, at least until the teacher's roving eye spotted our enterprise - and her eye had to rove along and across long desks with seventy to eighty children tightly squeezed in. 'Tables' were an exhausting physical activity that called for variety ... but we had to supply the variety.

Sometimes the class in the other half of the room chanted at the same time, and then it became a battle for survival. From the side room low noises were heard, steadily increasing in speed and intensity, matching our own ecstasy, until, fearful of losing sanity, the Headmistress would call to one of us, "Go and tell Miss Alice they are making too much noise."

There was quiet for a while - but only till the next round began.

The only apparatus I remember seeing was a bead-frame. It must have been ancient, for it was not easy to distinguish green from yellow or red from brown, and, as it stood so far away from us, as if it had been disowned. It was never used.

At a very tender age we had mastered the four rules and memorized some tables. At least we could manipulate numbers in certain ways, but it seemed like learning tricks. We did not really understand it.

To be released at playtimes was a doubtful pleasure. Into the small, earth-covered yard poured the infants and the pupils from the Girls' school at the opposite side of the yard. When groups of girls produced long ropes and began skipping, with a long line of girls running under the swinging rope, there was scarcely room for others to move. So we smaller infants pressed against the wall to avoid being knocked down by the mad creatures. At the age of three or four, boys as well as girls wore dresses, sometimes with a pinafore. In spite of the protection that long woollen stockings gave to our legs, a fall on the playground in winter spattered us with mud, dress and stockings being then fit for nothing but the wash tub.

* * * * *

The adventure of one afternoon shines out in my memory. During dinner mother mentioned that Mr. Bishop would be killing a pig that day. Quite a number kept pigs in sties built at the bottom of the back garden. Pork and bacon were a welcome supplement to the substantial diet so necessary to the miner, and orders were taken for pork for Sunday dinner and for the many other parts of the pig's anatomy that yielded luscious dishes, cold or hot. There were pig's cheek, feet, shanks, sweetbread, chitterlings, fry, liver and black pudding. Some of these were often distributed gratis to neighbours who had provided swill from their own kitchen scraps and refuse.

But for boys, killing a pig meant something else. For twopence we got the bladder, dried it carefully, inflated it by mouth, tied it securely - and there was a football. It was the bigger boys who usually laid claim to the bladder and we had the fun of watching. The strange thing about it was that it rarely travelled the direct course the kicker expected. There was the wild joy of chasing the unpredictable balloon ... until it burst, its life usually being brief.

I had not seen a pig killed and the prospect fascinated me. Dinner over, I wandered slowly across the Green to the back yard of my aunt's house, which was next to the place of slaughter. My aunt made sure that I remained on the safe side of the separating wall. When the piercing screams of the bleeding animal shattered my courage, I was calmly assured that it would soon all be over. And when a large bowl of warm, smoking blood was carried away, it was all over. I had had enough; it was time for me to go back to school.

I moved down the yard quietly (though not, I think, out of respect for the dying pig) into the back street, where I turned towards the Green. The place was deserted. What the hour was I did not know; no-one told me the time, so there I stood, a tiny, solitary figure in pinafore and dress, looking wonderingly around me. In the distance towered the tall, grim school gate. I had never been late; I did not know how to go there late. I could open neither gate nor door. Nor could I think of traversing alone that vast distance to the gate, with the eyes of housewives peering from behind their curtains, watching, wondering what that small boy was doing. So I changed my mind and crossed to our house. Where would mother be and what would be her reaction? Quietly I entered the kitchen. It was silent as death.

Just as silently I tiptoed across the floor and peeped under the large red, tasselled cloth that overhung the table. There was room and to spare, so in that house of quiet under the table, hidden by those hanging walls, I spent the rest of the afternoon. When the voices of children returning home from school enlivened the air, I forsook my hiding-place and joined them in the street.

It was some years later that I learned what playing truant was, and I saw and heard how it was punished. But my innocent adventure remained long untold, even to my mother.

*　*　*　*　*

In a church school it was considered important that little children should learn about God and Heaven, so each morning we stood in our long desks for the act of worship. First, though, it was impressed upon us that only when everyone was quiet, when you could hear a pin drop, could the service begin. We were told to stand nicely, no shuffling, no coughing, no sneezing, no kicking the iron supports of the desks, no scraping of feet on the floor, not a solitary sound, quiet as the quietest mouse. Then, after what seemed like an age, the pin dropped. The Headmistress really let a pin drop to the floor from the hand she held behind her back.

Someone actually heard it! Then everyone had heard it. When the first screamed "Yes, Miss," and shot his hand like an arrow into the air, another cried, "Yes, Miss," and shot up his hand, until the room rang with the cry. Miss turned to smile at Miss, and they beamed across the forest of hands quivering with excitement. In such a manner was solemn silence achieved and in such a manner was it shattered. Then we recovered our places in the desks and tried to stand still again, to be quiet again for the voice that spoke.

"Now, children, quiet again, quiet as a mouse" she whispered. "Put your hands together, close your eyes, and say after me ..." Then, phrase by phrase, we repeated The Lord's Prayer; with the silence flooding around us, we almost expected to see God dropping in upon us. (What this recitation meant, they never told us, yet we had to say it every day - afternoons as well - before we went home. We enjoyed saying it like that, though, all together.)

Then we sang a hymn. There was no piano, no harmonium, but Miss had a nice voice. She sang a line, we sang the same - or what we thought was the same - so that, by and by, we had learnt a whole verse. It took a time to learn the entire hymn, with only Miss to sing to us.

When that was over we sat in our places to listen to Miss telling us a story from the Bible. At least she said it was. I had my doubts.

Speaking for myself, I particularly disliked the one about two boys called Cain and Abel. One of them was good and one was bad. The bad one did not like his brother because of one day when they were both offering sacrifices to God. Abel was very pleased when he saw the smoke from his fire rising in a straight column to the skies. That, said teacher, showed that God was pleased with him. But the smoke from Cain's fire began to blow all round and never got up into the sky. Teacher said that was because he did not please God. Cain became very jealous of Abel and so angry that he killed him. I thought that was a horrible story. I would not kill my brother and I did not think that he would want to kill me.

It makes me shudder that such a tale should be told to little children. There were others, too, about fires and floods and plagues and battles. The darkness which shrouded the infancy of the human race was scarcely a subject in this guise for presentation to infant children and it is remarkable that, for so long, people responsible for education believed the religious instruction of young children should begin with the first pages of the Bible and wend its gory way through pages that only a well-educated person could effectively and sympathetically present. Few teachers were anywhere near prepared for a task that was far greater than they knew.

In retrospect it is horrifying to remember so vividly the wrong things told as the truth. I make no reproach, for Teacher was a very nice person. She never thought that some day some of us would discover other things about those stories.

CBEO

GOING UP

It was a great occasion when, on the morning of our return from the summer holiday, boys and girls were separated, checked, counted and finally marched across to the Big School, each to their separate Department. The Boys' section comprised one long room, divided by a partition of wood and glass, and one small room leading off from the lower half. As soon as the procession entered, excitement showed in a gentle murmuring of eager recognition by older brothers — no-one dared attempt a more audible demonstration. Like little pilgrims wandering towards the unknown we walked slowly along, silent and awe-struck, past three classes of juniors then two of seniors, whose amusement at the invading 'babies' could not be stifled.

We were told to stand between the rows of desks at the far end. How well I was to remember that corner of the school. That was the big boys' domain, where law and order were defied as frequently as they were enforced; where quarrels in class were temporarily subdued by agreements to fight outside; where the big door swung swiftly open as a victim fled without warning in protest against a severe hiding. Here, on the seats of the giants we sat, feet dangling from the long seats, awaiting the pleasure of our new masters.

We had not long to wait. There was no nonsense about how to deal with reception class on the first morning. The list of children had accompanied us, the register had been prepared, and marking began. For small boys from the infants school, accustomed to answering, "Yes, Miss," it came as a thunderclap to hear a masculine voice shout "Don't call me Miss - I'm not a Miss; say 'Sir'". We tried to say 'Sir' but after three years of saying 'Miss', Operation Register was irregular and prolonged, with not inaudible comments from the young master (in fact a pupil-teacher) about the products of the Infants School.

These comments became monotonously familiar as the years passed. The Junior School prided itself on what it did with what it got from below; the Grammar School was caustic about 'the best' they received from the Junior School; the Secondary Modern wondered how anything could be expected from ... "Well, you know what these are like". And finally the Employer, with the whole range of the educational system to choose from, including the universities, bewailed the same depressing scene. Perhaps the truth is that people forget how they themselves began to walk. They expect other folk to be born running.

But in that school on that Monday morning worse was to follow.

We were told to stand and pick up the slates and slate pencils the older boys had laid out for us. After being paired off we were told to turn sideways and stand back to back. This was our introduction to the morality of the big school. But holding in our arms the large slate, with a pencil to safeguard, and in such a confined space, we found ourselves in difficulties. Some of us turned the wrong way, some dropped the pencil, which fell down successive steps and came to rest only against the opposite wall, others jabbed the corner of the slate frame against the head or arm of a neighbour, occasioning a sudden shriek of pain. Gradually, however, order was restored, the impatient teacher grumbling volubly all the while about the haplessness of 'these infants'.

Only when calm prevailed could the next step be taken. With supreme confidence in the transparent simplicity of his instructions, the teacher began. This was a test in arithmetic, on the first morning after four fine weeks of careless rapture.

"Write down, as you have been taught, H T U. Now put these numbers underneath," after which he called out four numbers involving tens and units or hundreds, tens and units.

"Draw the lines for the answer, but don't put that in till I tell you."

"Number Two. Take twenty-seven from seventy-two."

How well I remember this sum! In all the ages it has been the fulfilment of desire in perverted teachers to "catch out" their witless pupils. Six years, seven, eight years old, some of them, I heard later, were nine years old, fresh from the Infants School.

And so it went on. The next was a times, or multiply, and the fourth was 'Divide'. With final instructions to get them all right and not to copy (which meant looking at someone else's work and writing down his figures) we were told to "Do these sums".

It did not take long, except for a few who never finished anything, and then, as we stood in an unfamiliar silence, the huge male crushed his way among us, filling us with a kind of fear that we had not known hitherto. With a piece of chalk he marked the sums, a tick for right and a cross for wrong.

His work finished, he quickly left the classroom, to fetch the Headmaster, it turned out.

As the great man approached - tall, authoritative from head to foot - it was obvious that something was wrong, seriously wrong.

"Send for the Headmistress", he called out with all his dread authority. The pupil-teacher ran the message himself and in seconds he was requesting the presence of the lady. The Headmaster wished to see her; it was 'Important'. In the meantime we stood there examining our slates. On mine were three ticks and a cross, the same as on my neighbour's. We gazed at each other, silently mystified. We used to get them all right. How had we got that one wrong?

Then entered the Headmistress. In our Infants School she had smiled at us and spoken so kindly, but here walked a different woman. Still erect but with fear in her eyes, she strode steadily past those long rooms to the corner where her latest flock stood huddled.

And HE turned to face her.

"Not one child got the subtraction right. What do you make of that?"

Dumb, quite dumb she stood. It was incomprehensible. How could it possibly be? She spoke quietly; there was little she could say. In a few, fleeting moments someone had passed judgement on the patient work of herself and her staff. Then she turned and walked away, dignified but scarcely serene.

How could she know that her little lambs had been thrown into confusion? "Take twenty-seven from seventy-two." They had never had a sum like that before. They had always been told the bigger number first and had written the numbers as they were called. And every one of us had done just that.

I have often wondered what was said that evening when the Headmaster returned home. He was the husband of the Headmistress!

The small classroom was our abode for a year. There we learned more sums, how to write 'compositions' - we could already write a cursive hand - and how to spell and read. At this time reading for pleasure was scarcely recognized; we learned to read because we had to be able to read. There was not a wide range of literature, only three or four 'readers', miscellaneous collections of stories (often with a moral) plus accounts of people and things that would nourish our infant minds. When we reached the end of the book, we started again at the beginning. There was no nonsense about it; we had to be able to read those books. Some of us could have read them backwards ... even blindfold, had we been put to the test.

From Standard One those who had made satisfactory progress went into Standard Two. Those who had not done so stayed in the first class. Standards Two, Three and Four were *all* accommodated in the Big Room. Whenever all the teachers decided to perform their tables at the same time, the noise defied description. Each of us fought for himself as he stood, and each class shouted to be heard above the din of its rivals. To write was peace, but not for long. It was a belief widely held in teaching circles in those days that if quiet prevailed, something was wrong. On tiptoe the Headmaster would steal along and shatter the silence with a bark that must surely have frayed the nerves of the unsuspecting teacher. Teacher must show that they were still awake, so they had to keep others awake.

The instrument of this principle was the cane - symbol of authority; goad to the indolent; pointer for the blackboard and any picture placed upon it; conductor's baton in singing lesson. Above all, an instrument of torture to be suffered for a host of offences - dirty hands, sums wrong, incorrect answers, giving no answer at all, talking when talking was not permitted, cheating, lying - the list was long.

Through all the days the cane ("the stick" it was usually called) was the most abiding thing the school could boast, embodying as nothing else did the element of permanence. It might fray through constant application, even break in use, but twopence spent at the local Post Office speedily replaced it, even in the course of a lesson. The institution of the cane vied with the Apostolic Succession in its claim to continuity through the ages.

The most distressing experience was to see a boy flogged mercilessly for sheer inability to do something he had been told to do - so much so that his cries filled the school. When shrieks gave way to long, low moaning, groaning and sobbing as if it would never end, he might be told to go and sit beside the fire, and when that failed to restore his comfort and his spirits, he would be given a penny. By that time he was in a mood to take anything. It was something not to talk about, and we kept our counsel.

That was the daily road to learning.

It was at this point in my life in a junior standard, at the age of seven, when a memorable incident occurred. Memorable because later in my career I became an official visitor to schools.

One morning I was lying on the couch at home. I was not well and mother had insisted I stay at home. There came a knock on the back door. Mother opened it and there saw one of my classmates.

"Please, the Headmaster wants to know if Teddy can come to school. The Inspector has come."

No Royal summons could have been obeyed with greater readiness. I had heard the message and before mother had returned to me I was off the couch and was putting on my boots.

"Do you think you are well enough to go?" she asked. Off I went. "THE INSPECTOR HAS COME". My presence was essential.

It is quite likely that I was not the only pupil missing that morning, and it is just as likely that the presence of some of them was neither desired nor sought. But my presence was required. Years later I understood. The Inspector had come to test every child in the school in reading, writing and arithmetic ... The Three Rs. The Headmaster's salary was at stake, for on the number of passes in these subjects throughout the school was based the Government Grant towards his salary. And I was good for four sums right, and I could read and spell. It would help if I could be counted in.

If, then, school was hard-driven and schooling a tough process, it was because the system known as Payment by Results debased teaching and those who taught against a background of fear - fear of the Inspector who held such power, fear of a threat to their livelihood. And, what made it worse, the assessor had perhaps never taught anything in his life! A small boy, asked specially to leave a sick couch to save the Headmaster's salary! I have never forgotten.

But there were times of happy relief in this grim process of learning. For oral lessons two classes were squeezed together into the desks of one and in that solid mass we experienced security even in discomfort. Facing that sea of faces the Headmaster (a new one) taught us Geography. To this day I remember that Oakham is the county town of Rutland. Every county town of every county in England and Wales had to be known. The name, too, of every river down the east coast, along the south and up the west became a song of running waters.

Swale, Ure, Nidd, Wharfe, Aire, Calder, Don and Derwent - with this rhythmic pattern we memorized the rivers flowing into the Humber, chanting loudly as the master tapped out the rhythm with the cane on the front desk.

The capes and bays round the coast likewise made a fascinating list. There was Beachy Head and Dungeness, The Lizard and Land's End, with Ardnamurchan Point the most mysterious and captivating of all. But they were only names, with never a picture to show Spurn Head's sandy spit, low in the grey North Sea, or the volcanic rocks of the western capes withstanding the rolling breakers of the Atlantic. There was no teaching without memorization, and when I grew interested in First Division Football I knew, at any rate, where those illustrious teams had their homes.

The teaching, though, had its limitations. It is remarkable how one remembers the wrong things; for instance, that the indented coast of West Scotland, like that of Norway, was due to erosion by the sea.

The school had not yet opened its windows to science for young and lively people. Instead we were treated to 'Object Lessons', in which our thought and attention were directed (as if they needed to be) to objects animate and inanimate, such as the horse, cow, sheep and cat, holly and mistletoe, cotton and wool If sometimes the facts were familiar, the explanations were less obvious, and so began the quest for knowledge about the world around us. New wonders were catching our attention, as when a neighbour played an Edison phonograph for us, with voices and music coming from a cylindrical wax record; the motor car, whose noise and hideous horn startled horses in the street so that they dashed away our of control, and the monoplane of the Wright Brothers flying through the air gave a new dimension to our lives. (Little did I realize that in years to come I would actually be driving a motorcar or, beyond all dreams, piloting a plane across wartime skies.) If school lagged behind the thrilling world with its fiction coming true, it was because the law demanded that pupils should first be proficient in the three R's. Let the great world go by!

Art was a word that was not then in the vocabulary of schools. A drawing lesson did however have its place on the timetable, and we drew with a black lead pencil. On each desk was one India-rubber, for joint use; it could well have been described as a scrubber. On the blackboard was pinned a Drawing Card showing some symmetrical figure like a vase. We had to try to copy it, but symmetry was difficult to achieve. One side invariably became swollen, and if efforts at rubbing out and trying again resulted eventually in a crater in the paper, the penalty made drawing not an enjoyable experience. Nor was the pleasure enhanced when you were told to look at a wooden cube, dust-covered, upon a table at the front of the class. You was expected to note how the top and bottom edges 'vanished' only to meet at some indefinite distance, which had not to be shown on the paper, on an invisible line known as the 'eye level'. To a boy of eight it was fantastic nonsense and one had a peculiar pleasure in scorning it. If they had taken us out of school to see lines 'vanishing' in the long streets, or to the railway crossing, it would all have come to life. But a vanishing cube! I always wondered why it lived a solitary life on the cupboard top.

In those junior standards we young boys learned to survive the unceasing combat between the teacher's wits and ours, and between each other - an equally hard struggle intellectually and physically - but for me it was great fun.

 CBSO

BIG SCHOOL

The time was near when events would change the habits and lives of people. For long we had been used to the bright red glare of the furnaces by night and the clanging sounds of the mills by day. Then came the news that the ironworks were to close down; parts of it were to be transferred to another centre, other parts were to be scrapped. No high-sounding words like 'redundancy': men were simply 'out of work'. There was no 'dole' to draw; that came in later on. The inquisition for Parish Relief was pitiless and as a result few sought it. Men stood at street corners, sad, dejected creatures, the reddish-brown dust still showing on their heavy boots and loose clothes. Nothing could be had on the slate; their thirst must go unquenched; there was not even money for food.

It was almost 1892 all over again, without the bitterness of strife. Then the miners knew the pits would open again, but this time there was no such hope. Children came to school bootless or with the soles through. By voluntary efforts soup kitchens were opened, miners and others sending potatoes, turnips, leeks, cabbages and anything they had to spare from their gardens.

The Head figured prominently in this relief work. Each morning in school he made out a number of cards bearing a name and address, and at half-past eleven he gave them to me. I knew where the folk lived and it became my job to run across the Green and hand the tickets to the women of those houses. At twelve o'clock they presented themselves at an improvised kitchen in the church hall with huge basins and bowls. These were filled with rich, thick soup, accompanied by a piece of bread, and there they had the main meal for the day.

How delicious that soup smelled. But I was glad our family escaped that hardship. For a long time the district was quiet with the silence that distress inflicted. Only slowly did men leave for other jobs and other places. There was no longer any 'chucking out' of the pubs, since few could afford to go in.

At the age of eleven I was buying and selling stocks and shares with incredible ease - in theory, that is. We never had sums on Co-op dividends, though, whereas the only arithmetic I did at home was when mother took out her Store bills for groceries, meat and draperies and asked me to find the totals and then calculate the amounts due at the different rates of dividend. How necessary it was to check became apparent when the office total was shown in the book to be less than my totals. When our bills were produced at the Store, the mistakes were corrected and the adjusted dividends placed to our credit. In that way I discovered commonsense arithmetic, in contrast to the hideous complex fractions that were so prominent in the unintelligible weight of school arithmetic books. And those dreadful, meaningless sums about decimals, with products to seven or eight places! No-one told us the sense of it: perhaps they never knew. Surely there was a better way to calculate those tiresome products and quotients! But that was a mathematical mystery to be revealed in due time and in other places.

It was at this stage of learning that the bigger boys openly rejected the traditional way of treating inaccurate solutions and confused mental processes. Before the lesson, as an essential instrument, the stick was placed on the desk. There it lay for all to see. That was in store for failure. Generally punishment was accepted, but only as part of a toughening process and never with any sense of justice.

There were times, though, when, with a course of action already determined, a boy would go forward at the teacher's command, glancing at the door as he went, and planning his escape route between blackboards and other obstacles and the door. Then, when he considered he had had enough, and resenting further measure, he shouted defiance, turned on his heels, dodged the obstacles, seized the door handle and pulled the massive door towards him, shouting as he fled from the room. We would see him leap the wall outside the window, and in our minds we saw him racing across the Green. Consternation prevailed, then we were told to get on with our sums.

His angry father appeared later.

There were no 'streams' or 'age groups' then. If a pupil's progress was slow, he stayed in the class as nearly suited to his attainment as possible. Big, resentful boys sat among small boys not long out of Infant school. Young boys who made good progress moved up the school. At eleven I was in the top class, among the heavyweights.

Apart from the battlefield of the arithmetic lesson, life was full of interest and some lessons were thoroughly enjoyable.

Some years ago I saw an old classmate who called across the street. "Come and talk about the old days! Do you remember this?" After fifty years he could remember with a thrill poems we had learnt together. So many people find poetry dull and some say that children should not be compelled to memorise it, but here was a man who experienced a great thrill in sharing such a recollection.

It was true we had to learn. But the pace was slow. Each week eight lines of verse were written on the blackboard, which, at half-past eleven, was reversed for us to see. "As soon as you can say that, you may go," said the teacher. Within minutes some of us knew it. Out to the front we went, said our piece and, when he uttered his curt, "Right. Go", fled the room. Twenty-five minutes more for play.

Alas for me: only too often was I deprived of that pleasure. The greater part of the class took much longer and by ten to twelve the queue was beyond the power of one man to hear. My reward was, "Right. Now you stay and hear some of the rest."

Other weeks we left early if we could say two verses, or three, or four, and so it went on. Little wonder that fifty years later those poems could still be recited, and with such enjoyment.

There were singing lessons too, though no such lessons as 'music'. Mysterious letters *d r m f s l t d'* were scattered along a line between short vertical strokes and dots like colons and separated sometimes by dashes. It all seemed weird until one learned the sounds associated with the letters in the form of a scale. Later we found there were fantastic complications to master. This is how we learned to sing.

First we read the letters *'m m m f f s f m r m f s d f m r d'*. Then we sang the sounds indicated by the letters again and again until they were firmly established. Then we sang them to the appropriate rhythm. Next, we said after the teacher the actual words of the line. Then we sang the words to the melody so laboriously learnt. And so on to the end of the verse. It took a long time to learn one song, but the Code for Elementary Schools required only that five national songs should be learnt in one year.

The only musical instrument in the school was an old harmonium. We had never heard it played. Shortly before one lesson, however, the Head called me and suggested I should accompany the class in one of the songs, "The Farmer's Boy", since he knew I had had lessons from my father. The harmonium lid was lifted and folded back, the dust of ages blown away, the keys wiped with the cloth blackboard duster, to become soft white upon ivory black, and I sat on the chair, the only chair in the school. (It is important to remember that no teacher ever sat during lessons. It simply was never done.)

Feet on the pedals I pressed to fill the bellows. Then, before my hands could touch the keys, strange sounds issued forth as if a ghostly performance were within. When I tried to play, some of the keys struck and sustained, discordant sounds filled the room. This was not "The Farmer's Boy" but "The Farmer's Yard", at early morn too. So we never had the pleasure of singing that song with full accompaniment on harmonium. That was the end of its day. And tonic-solfa long reigned victorious, happy and glorious.

For Scripture, as Religious Instruction was then called, we were taught the catechism of the Church of England, together with lessons based on Old and New Testaments. This was inculcated very faithfully and strictly according to the Time Table, which provided for a daily period. Each Wednesday morning the Vicar or the Curate gave us older boys instruction. The latter was frequently a new arrival, and it soon became obvious to us that he was learning to teach. It was to our credit that we treated him with great respect, even when his questions, so strangely worded, proved impossible to answer. However, a 'proper' teacher was always present in the room to supervise, and a glance from him was sufficient to restore order.

The visit of the Vicar created a stir. When this tall, bearded figure - draped in black, with his black cape visibly enlarging his presence – entered, the stir ceased and a most respectful silence fell upon the room. His slow, dignified progress was followed with awe and wonder. There was a pause in the battle, the stick was laid aside, and we heard of Charles the First or the flood waters of the Ganges or a subordinate or adjectival clause in tones that suggested so persuasively that these were lofty matters for our thought and edification. But I was 'chapel', and his person seemed always remote to me.

The best thing about him, I thought, was when we went to church on Ascension Day and sang: "*Up in heaven, up in heaven, In the bright land far away,*" and he told us that the rest of the day was to be a holiday. At such times he seemed so nice, that I could not understand why the words "The Vicar", were whispered in tones of near dread; it seemed unreal to me, him being the representative of the Church and I thought he might sometime be interested in pupils, but he never got as far as that, not even with those who attended his church and Sunday School. He left the weekly teaching to the curate, who did show an interest.

For the Head, though, the Vicar's visit must have been important. It was a relief to him and to the other teachers when the boy who had been holding his horse outside the school gate came back into school and said with all the pride of superior knowledge, "Please, sir, he's gone now." Even the teachers found it a little awkward to abandon courtesy and restraint and join battle once more. The tough ones among us chuckled that there would be no more stick that afternoon.

Another event of the week that had special importance was the visit of the "kid-catcher". The Head left his class with work to do, proceeded to his desk, and there, with the registers of all the classes, they examined the state of absenteeism. Not the state of attendance. It was the absent ones who were his concern.

The "kid-catcher" was a person to avoid, which we tried to do at all times, even weekends. If, suddenly, as we were playing on the Green, the cry went up "Kid-catcher", we fled into hiding ... in the back yard, behind a cree, a wall, anywhere to escape his eye. Even the ball was allowed to roll away wherever it might go; we would find it again. It was useless, though. He had seen us: he always saw everyone. He knew everyone, and should he see any scholar out of school when he was aware that that person should be in school, the chase began. Hence his name, "Kid-catcher". To be hauled before him in school, to account for an absence previously unexplained, was a frightening experience, except for those who could never be frightened anyhow. Their fathers had told them he couldn't do anything to harm them, but most of us thought it better not to take the risk.

The regular absences of girls on certain days or half-days posed a special problem. If Tuesday was washday, it was decreed in some families that the eldest girl should stay at home to help with the washing. The kid-catcher knew the homes and sometimes he visited while the child was in the act of assisting. Then ensued an argument over the poss-tub and the soapsuds that was anything but edifying. A woman who had to wash shirts, pants, stockings and anything else of her miner-husband and sons - two, three, four or more - in a steam-filled kitchen with poss-tub and old-style iron mangle prominent upon the floor, was a formidable adversary to confront with sleeves rolled above the elbow as she thumped, thumped with the huge poss-stick in the steaming tub, standing waist-high. And he could wait, she told him, till she had - thump ... thump - finished. Then, what did he want?

But the K.C. of those defiant days had the law on his side. He needed it, too, for his own preservation.

Fridays and Friday afternoons, too, saw a big drop in attendance, with brasses on the mantelpiece to polish, steel fender and fire irons to shine bright, the andiron and the tidy to clean. It was a fierce ritual, the fireside transformed to a sparkling altar, and the high priestess brooked no interference with age-long custom. There were floors to wash, outside steps to clean and edge with a white or yellow clay for a distinctive touch, and the yard to swill. On it went, swish and scrub, till, wet and exhausted, they declared that was enough for this time.

On another satisfying level there was bread to be baked, probably teacakes too, and this could be the crown of the woman's week. To share in this was a girl's delight, an illegitimate one, but, contrasted with spellings and dictation, heaven. Nor were the boys averse to a part in the domestic festival. On alternate Fridays a boy might be sent to fetch father's pay (father being asleep in bed) or on a score of errands that seemingly could only be done on a Friday afternoon - to take the order for groceries, to fetch the groceries, to borrow from auntie or to repay something that had been borrowed. A fortnight was a long time to make a pay-packet spin out, and some were not expert at it. Sometimes even the experts in frugality failed. It was a life that demanded mathematical skill to manipulate what was not there; an occasional absence from school mattered less to them than the absence of food from the table. They fought for their own priorities.

Over the fortunes and misfortunes of life at school the kid-catcher's spectral form hung like doom. The Vicar came and saw and went. The kid-catcher was a perpetual presence, the nightly threat of parents to a wayward child. We wondered that anyone should actually seek to do a job that incurred so much odium and gave little apparent pleasure.

*   *   *   *   *

When the weather was fine we were often released from the crush of the schoolyard to play on the Green. Occasionally the Head and staff entertained us with a demonstration of a game played by men and attracting large crowds when experts were matched. This was Handball, differing from fives in being played against one wall only, and not three.

The long, high, windowless stone wall facing the Green gave excellent facility for this game. The ball used was a 'thick indy' and the game was played by two opponents or two pairs.

The area of the wall on which the ball was to be knocked was defined at one side by the drainpipe that led the rainwater off from the roof, and at the other by the end of the wall. Between these limits and about three feet from the ground a line was chalked; if the ball struck the wall below that line it became 'dead' and the point counted against the striker. The area of the playing space was indicated by lines drawn on the ground from the two ends of the wall space.

Play was begun by striking the ball with the hand or fist or by throwing the ball against the wall area. It was struck in return by an opponent, and striking continued in turn until one player failed to return the ball correctly into the wall area, driving, for instance, below the line or beyond the side limits.

Great excitement prevailed when we saw that the Head and three teachers were going to play and nearly the whole school stood round to watch. With his keen, penetrating eyes set beneath jet black, slightly curled brows and hair, the Head fascinated us. He moved as one with a purpose, jerking his shoulders as he walked with a confident intent. When he took a lesson, learning was a pleasure and teaching an art. Now, on the Green, he showed us another realm in which he shone. He was rather heavily built and he made up for being slower than the younger teachers by hard drives, accurately placed just above the line and which, rebounding rather low, were difficult to return.

When others panted through lack of breath or perspired with running to and fro - forward to the low drive, backward to the high, ballooning ball far out from the base - he remained cool and calm, as in everything he did. Watching the others we became aware of the limitations of some of our teachers, but we looked on in keen appreciation. These were the men who "tanned the hide off us", and here we saw another side of their lives. They were not perfect but they were human, our daily foes and friends.

Too often it has been thought that in a boys' school the way to bring them up is to "treat 'em rough." Whatever refinement existed here emanated from the personality of the Head himself, and long after one left school, one remembered him for his fairness, for his respect for us, and for his courtesy. He was essentially a gentleman, his innate kindness and quiet strength gaining everyone's admiration.

*　*　*　*

The twenty-ninth of May
Royal Oak Day
If you don't give us holiday,
We'll all run away.

This was sung at school during the morning playtime on the 29th. That the holiday would be given was a wild dream, but the wilder element once decided to take it. Entering the school during dinner hour they secured the key of the big door and locked it. Then off they went to the river, three miles away, where with great excitement the key was thrown into a deep pool. The rest of the afternoon was spent in lively fashion in the river, along the banks and in attempting the adventurous traverse of the crude stepping-stones

At school next morning the inquisition took place, first for the truancy and second for the missing key, and the penalties were duly paid in the customary manner. The school had functioned normally, for there was more than one door to the school. If there was any satisfying feature in connection with the incident it was that the teachers had an easier afternoon with smaller classes.

It was at this point that there came the chance to leave school. Those who had reached twelve years of age and were in Standard Four, or a higher class, could enter the Labour Examination in Arithmetic and English. If successful they were awarded a Labour Certificate, which entitled them to seek employment. Those who did not sit or who were unsuccessful had to remain at school till they were fourteen years old.

I sat and passed, but I never even asked for my certificate. My parents had never considered my leaving. Evidently they could manage without the few shillings a week I could have brought in, and one thing in their minds was certain - I was not going "to the pit."

For those who left there was little but the coalmines and I thought, even then, how unfortunate it was that they had no other opportunities for different work. At the pits beginners were set to work "on the belts". It was on the belts that the newly-mined coal was tipped, and as the belts moved remorselessly along, the boys, spaced at intervals, frantically picked out the pieces of stone mixed with the coal and threw them into the boxes provided. For that they were paid four or five shillings a week: that was the first step in coal-mining. When they met us at the weekend, they looked on us with a sense of superiority, men in the making, their pride of status showing in the coal-dust rings round their eyes, which for a while they were not too particular to remove in washing.

Highlight of the school at this time was the last lesson on Friday afternoon, not because four o'clock brought us liberty for the weekend, but because from three-thirty to four we listened to a story, one chapter each week. That was a pleasure too far spaced out; that was the only fault. In contrast to everything else he gave us to do in the rest of the week, here the teacher chose wisely. Bobby, acknowledged by everyone to be the best, most dramatic reader, had the honour of reading and we listened spellbound. Occasionally I was called on to relieve him. This was no attempt to edify the listeners; it was simply sheer enjoyment. At a time when interesting boys' books were few, that introduction to the joys of literature was to be long remembered.

There came a day when a great shadow fell across our end of the school. The number of children seeking admission to the infants' school increased so considerably that the church hall had to be taken over to house additional classes. Then, to make room for children awaiting transfer to the big school, the top class was told that after the summer holiday they must attend another school - there was no longer room for them here. I was one of those who had to move.

Two schools were nearby - one a Wesleyan School, the other a comparatively new building, a Board School controlled by the School Board set up by the Education Act of 1870. It was said that its top class was under a very capable teacher. My parents decided that I should go to the Board School.

C3ED

1. Miners at Tudhoe Grange Colliery c1900 (Tom Roberts (father) on extreme right)

2. Mount Pleasant School, c.1899? - Edward Roberts on front row, extreme right

3. Some of the Roberts family in front of their music shop, early 1900s

4. Spennymoor Baptist Church Bible Class, c1908: Ed Roberts extreme right

5. Spennymoor Baptist Church football team, 1910-11: Ed Roberts 2nd from left on back row

7. Edward Roberts on Graduation Day

6. Tom & Rachel Roberts

8. The Roberts family in the early 1920s

9. Edward Roberts in later life

TATIE PICKING

One particular fine Saturday morning in October I woke feeling that this was going to be a great day. I dressed and went out into the street to play. It was only half-past seven, and the early starters for work were moving off with a briskness that the keen air stimulated.

There was little fun in playing alone and in a kick of annoyance I sent the ball farther along the road than I anticipated. I chased after it when, dashing from the corner before I could reach it, there came Jimmie. A large pail was slung over his head to rest on his back, the hoop circling his neck. I marvelled at such alacrity under such a handicap. But Jimmie was celebrated for his speed and ease of movement. With a ball at his feet he could turn as on a pinhead. If there was a hole in a wall or fence that was too small for others to pass through, Jimmie could wriggle it, even a needle's eye. He took a leap in the air and with a terrific kick sent the ball, not back along the road, but over the wall into the churchyard. As good as lost, I thought, looking at the long grass that the sexton had failed to cut.

But Jimmie was equal to the occasion. "Come on, lads, help look for the ball," he called. From round the corner came a dozen lads, all from school, all carrying a zinc pail their mothers had spared to them — or would miss an hour later. Over the wall they jumped. They were accustomed to looking for lost balls. They often found more than they were looking for. But this time to find my ball was all to be done.

They had work to do: They were going potato-picking and suggested I should go with them when the ball was found.

"But I haven't got a pail," I said.

"There'll be spare pails on the field. You'll be all right."

So I joined the ranks there and then - with good boots on my feet, nothing on my head, and with no breakfast and without a word to anyone at home - I vanished into the lane.

The farmer's wife was the boss, a tiny, wizened creature, hard-skinned, hard-hearted and with a tongue that scalded. For lack of

45

anything else to drive, her tall, match-stick husband drove the horses. No one ever heard him speak, not even the horses. He swung pendulum-like as he strode with vast steps over the earth.

She saw us enter the field.

"You're late!" she yelled. "Come on, get a start! The row's ready."

The farmer had already turned the first row of ripened plants and the earth had fallen to expose the potatoes. It was our job to pick all we could see and delve deeply and quickly with the hands for any that might still lie covered by the soil. In quick succession you picked, picked, picked, dropping each potato into the pail until it was full. Then you carried the pail to a sack placed in the row, emptied it into the sack, and the filled sack awaited the farmer's collection.

She saw I was slow. She knew me, too; she left milk at our house.

"I thought you said you had been out before," she hurled at me. "You've got to be faster than that. Look at the others. Does your mother know you've come?"

"Yes," I replied politely.

"Then why didn't she give you a pail?"

I decided I had not heard that and ran along the row, shouting to Jimmie who was harvesting potatoes with the speed of an expert.

But it was miserable work. I had read in a paper about a preacher who spoke about the dignity of labour, yet I could see no dignity in this, floundering about in the earth above the ankles, pulling myself up and slithering down again, feet astride and body bent from the waist, arms shooting down to seize hold of the potatoes and as in one movement to throw them into the pail, and every few seconds lift the pail to have it nearer, on and on and on, down and up, down and up, along the never-ending line. The lads enjoyed it. They shouted all kinds of funny remarks until little Liz told them to get on with the job.

Mid-morning came, and on we bent and rose. My nose started to bleed, my back ached, my feet were damp and my hands were cold. Now missing my breakfast, I was hungry and miserable. But I had volunteered for this experience, and if David Livingstone could travel through Darkest Africa, I could survive the morning in a potato field.

The morning. We all thought the same: we only wanted to work the morning. There was a football match in the afternoon. We always went to the match on Saturday afternoon. We could not miss that.

Twelve o'clock. Time to stop.

"Can we have our money now, Missis? We're not coming back this afternoon."

"Aren't you now?" she almost sang. "Well then, no pay for anybody who doesn't come back this afternoon. So that's it. Please yourselves."

It was no use arguing. We had lost.

When I walked into the house for dinner, there was amazement, consternation and laughter. The general feeling was that it would do me good.

I must have eaten twice the amount of a usual dinner when the shouting of the returning column took me from the table. There was only one topic of conversation as we walked the road to the field - the mean creature who denied the lads their Saturday football match.

We all felt much better as we began the afternoon shift. From the distance came the triumphant shouts of the crowd as a goal was scored, and our fancy winged to see our top forward in full flight.

Five o'clock came with fading light and chill air. It had been a great day, despite a backache, a bleeding nose and a hard boss.

Then we lined up to be paid, standing respectfully, thinking she might give us a bit extra. Jimmie was first. She handed him his money.

"What's this?" he asked, holding out his hand with a sixpence resting on the palm. He was very experienced and knew the rate for the job. "You've only given me sixpence, sixpence for a whole day. That's not right."

"It's exactly right," said Liz. "Men and women get a shilling a day. Half pay for boys. Sixpence, that's right."

A chorus of growling and shouting failed to change her mind.

"We'll take a pail of potatoes, then," was the cry. This was a general custom, a shilling a day and a pail of potatoes.

"Oh, no. No potatoes. If you don't want your money, don't take it."

Defeated on every hand we took our sixpences and walked the lane disconsolately, sadness and anger weighing us down.

When I gave mother my sixpence, she smiled kindly. She knew I had learned one lesson. I never went potato-picking again.

ᘓᕲᘔᕴ

FOOTBALL ON THE GREEN

The Green was our football pitch. We played soccer there all year round.

It was an area undefined by white lines. From end to end the limits were seen in the two goals. Instead of goal posts heaps of broken bricks and stones were piled to mark the width of the goal. If these were not obtainable, the more reckless lads took off their jackets and threw them on the ground at the appropriate places. Some of us had to think twice about being reckless. It had been dinned into us so often that clothes cost money that to throw a jacket wilfully on to the earth, dry as it might be, was sacrilege. We could not have gone home with such guilt on our mind. And someone would certainly have seen us and reported the matter before we got home.

The sidelines were invisible and intangible, in the mind rather than on the ground. In the back street was a gutter or channel, which could have been a line, and along the line were the outdoor closets and coalhouses separated from the houses themselves by the back street. If the ball was kicked on to this half built-up area, it was a chance for the skilled dribbler and cunning strategist to race round these obstacles and mystify his opponent as to where he might again be visible. Beyond this area towards the middle of the Green stood the black, tarred crees where hens and pigeons were raised. These, too, were obstacles that diverted the ball, sometimes excitingly to one's advantage, sometimes frustratingly.

There was no referee. We had our own code. When hands were used flagrantly to interfere with the ball's flight, we yelled "Hands". The ball was seized and a free kick taken. If the offence occurred near the goal, a penalty was demanded. This might be hotly disputed and some time would elapse before the rights of the situation were finally accepted. On occasion there were angry scenes and the game had to be abandoned. Mind you, there were few fouls. After all they were friendly games and any obviously bad offence was infrequent. But if it

48

did occur, it provoked speedy reaction and the victim struck up for a fight. When peace was restored and honour satisfied, a free kick was gained. It was a tribute to the general good sportsmanship of the boys that the attempt at self-government was largely successful.

No time was kept for changing ends. No-one had a watch. We changed when we thought it would help even things out, especially when a strong wind was blowing from one end to the other.

Teams were chosen on the spot. From the assembled boys two would be asked to select sides, one of them generally the owner of the precious ball. In turn each called out the name of a boy, and the boy named would take his place behind the captain till the teams were built up. Then they tossed for choice of end. 'Tossing' consisted usually in wetting the palm of one hand, after turning to conceal the operation, then holding out the two palms facing downwards, and calling for the choice 'Wet' or 'Dry' to be made.

The Ball! A real leather football was every boy's dream. To get one kick at a real football was something to talk about. There was one kept in school solely for the occasional match between neighbouring schools, and if the ball was kicked out of touch or past the goal line, there invariably took place a scramble to retrieve the ball for the proud pleasure of the chance to kick it. That was something to talk about and the momentary thrill to imagine oneself on a First Division side incited by a cheering crowd made one forget one's filthy boots. The urge to kick was in every boy's feet, so he kicked the ground, the wall, the gate, an empty salmon tin (that was quite light), a discarded treacle tin (that was heavy, too hard on the boots) and when nothing better was available, a stocking stuffed hard, very hard, with paper and waste wool and tied with string for security, was an object that would stand hard kicking ... for a while at least, but its track over the ground was erratic.

To own a real ball was terrific. For twopence you could buy an india-rubber ball at the newsagent's. Such wealth drew a host of friends as if by magic. At other times four boys, having come into a fortune through the various operations that boys knew about, would each put in a halfpenny, and off to the shop they would go. Old Mrs. Jennifer would don her spectacles for this important transaction, look carefully at the box of balls in the window, select one and place it on the counter.

Lennie felt it. "It's soft," he said. "No use, it'll burst straight away."

Mistakenly she replied, "They're all the same." "We'll go somewhere else then," Len answered, and they all raced off to shop number two.

"What do you think we are?" was the cry of disgust when the same trick was tried.

At shop number three they were met honestly and given good value for their money. With great excitement the whole crowd, now swollen at the prospect, rushed back to the Green, the boy with the ball leading the way.

With unexpected wealth someone would rise to buying a 'thick indy' for sixpence. There was really long life in this. It withstood hard kicking and kicking against a wall, it was fast through the air and a real 'stinger' for a goalkeeper to stop when a hard drive came from a sure foot. It was a very useful ball for cricket, too.

One evening as we kicked a ball about in a very ordinary game, I was confronted by a small chap who was in the same class as me. That morning we had had a row during the arithmetic lesson, when he accused me of looking at his slate for his answers. Copying? I sat in the row behind him. I could easily look over at his slate, but I had no need to. After all, the best scholars were in the back row, where I sat, and I resented the accusation and told him so. But he picked the quarrel and said, "Right. I'll fight you tonight on the Green."

There we were. He had come for his fight. And before the lads could realize what was happening, we were fighting. I felt it was unfortunate that he was smaller than I, but he asked for it and he got it. At any rate, he was my own age. The game broke off, we were enclosed by the shouting mob, my challenger was on the ground, when with scythe-like arms a red-haired figure cleared the ring, seized me roughly with her long arms and, looking down at me from her great height, she cried in scathing tones, "You should be ashamed of yourself, fighting a boy when his mother's died."

That stopped the fight. She seized her nephew and dragged him off to console him as best as her protective role would allow. I was sorry about his mother being dead. It did not appear to enter his thoughts when he challenged me. I did not hate him but what could I do? The incident fizzled out and there was no more talk of copying.

There were often fights like that. They made us tough. The worst was when some silly girl ran across the Green to tell somebody's mother that there was a fight. It spoilt things. The punishment was to have to stay indoors.

But the toll on one's boots! Constant kicking against the ground and the embedded stones wore the right toe through, broke the stitching of the toe-cap, stripped the sole or wore a hole through, even to the stocking. To go home with the tattered remains of boots ingloriously hanging from the feet was a sight to break the heart of mothers who daily tried to make one and one into three, and a sight to rouse fathers to seize a strap and apply it to the posterior of the young footballer with as much vigour as he exerted at the coal face.

For some of us it became almost a moral offence to indulge in any form of play that injured the home in the struggle for decent existence. Instinct said, "Kick." Home said, "It's a struggle as it is, without you kicking your boots to pieces."

I was sixteen before my mother bought me a real pair of football boots. A young minister had come to the chapel and he had the bright idea to form a football team for the young men's Bible Class. Mother would do anything when it was for the chapel. That was how I got my first pair, and they lasted a long time.

Albert got his in a way much more heroic.

His feet sang with the urge that was in him, and his father did his best to end the song. Mother too. Did they not already do sufficient to buy boots to wear for school? He would be the ruin of them. The strap failed to cure him. Being sent to bed failed too. They bought him clogs to wear in the evening. But who could play football in clogs?

So the ball was at his feet. He must solve his own problem. Returning from Grammar School one afternoon he noticed in a shop window a fascinating display of football boots. In the centre rested a junior ball, and round it, like spokes of a wheel, boots of varying sizes with block toes, white pigskin uppers and studded soles — price three shillings, eleven and a half pence per pair. His mind whirled with the possibilities. He would buy a pair. He would pay for them himself. He would work and save every penny and halfpenny until at last a pair of those shoes shone on his feet. He could see already goals, goals, goals all the way. He would show them what a boy could do.

Pocket-money was no good; it would take ages. He took thought.

Now it has to be understood that the free load of coal that miners received was generally tipped just outside the coal-house, across the back street. The men were not always at home when the coal was delivered and women were not always inclined to do it. But for boys this was a real money-raiser. Albert looked along the street for fresh loads to put in and ran to offer his services.

A penny to put a load in: one solitary penny.

So precious were pennies, both to the boy who sold his labour and the housewife who bought it. For a bigger load one and a half pence. And if by mistake the coal had been wrongly dumped, and carrying a pail at a time was involved, the payment was tuppence, two pence for a job that left him as black as the coal itself. But it was money earned. It was his own.

And sometimes a load was sold. It was against the rules but there were times when cash in hand was to be preferred to a coal-house filled to the roof. If a wheel-barrow had to be used, the reward was thruppence for what was a man's work.

A second source of finance was in running errands for neighbours. This had been established as a weekly practice, every Saturday morning, to help neighbours who had no family. Two houses sought Albert's help to fetch their groceries from the Co-op. For carrying two large parcels, slung round his shoulders through the belt off his Norfolk jacket, unknown to his mother, he was paid one penny. Three halfpence if it was raining.

Then his father began to co-operate. He would not give money, but he would help him to earn it. Out of a bacon-box, strong substantial timber in those days, he made a bogey, a box on wheels, with strong shafts, so that from the streets and the lanes he could gather horse manure, so freely strewn by horses at that time and so acceptable to gardeners. Dad was a gardener. It was slow, hard work. In the course of a week he would gather three or four loads and his father paid him a penny a load. In this realm of coal and errands and manure the penny held sovereign sway.

As each coin was dropped into the box, Albert counted. Then came the day when with a shout he proclaimed, "I've got it!" Three shillings and eleven and a half pence!

On fleet foot he dashed to the shop in the High Street. The display had been dismantled but the shoes were there, and the ticket said "Three shillings and eleven and a half pence." Glorious sight!

He walked in and breathlessly gave his order. "I want that pair of football boots, three shillings and elevenpence hapenny, please."

The manager honoured the boy with his personal attention. It was a rare sight, a boy buying for himself. He reached for a pair to which Albert pointed.

"Yes," he said, "these are three and eleven and a half pence, but," and he looked at Albert's huge feet, "these are too small for you. Your size costs four shillings and three pence ha'penny."

Albert felt himself shrinking smaller and smaller. There was no card in the window marked four and thruppence ha'penny.

He wished the floor would open. The disappointment was devastating. He was a few coppers short, but to be short was to be without. It was to have nothing.

He crawled home, heart and limbs heavy as lead. The coins were light in his pocket. There was not sufficient.

He passed through the kitchen without a word. No one saw his face. In the back yard sat his collie. He sat beside him and, as if he knew his plight, the dog licked his cheek.

Then in moments the scene changed. There came one to whom he was the apple of her eye. His aunt saw his misery, and drawing him from the caressing dog, asked, "Have you got those football boots yet?" He could neither look up nor answer.

Then followed words he was longing to hear. "Get your money and we'll go down the street."

He deserved them, really and truly.

Those were hard days for getting luxuries like football boots.

ભ્રૠ

THE HARD WAY

Before the change took place, a great upheaval occurred in our lives. For over a year father had been in poor health. To continue working in the mine would aggravate his trouble and so an important decision had to be taken. In a community offering little choice of other employment the individual was left entirely to his own devices. There were no such things as Employment Exchanges; if you were without a job, you were without means of subsistence. To have a wife and family to support could cause serious hardship in such circumstances.

The plunge was taken. We bought a house and shop not far away, on Half Moon Lane. Father's interest in music would have an outlet, for he would sell musical instruments and take on more pupils for the piano and organ. There could be no luxury in such a life, but there was independence and that would be maintained.

Despite the tremendous change in the home and the uncertainty that was bound to prevail for a time, I was allowed to stay at the new school. We children were not kept together, but after an examination were dispersed into various classes. I found myself in the top class.

It was fortune undreamed. For so long I had endured as normal the noise and distractions of several teachers and classes in one long room; now here I was in a small class in a small room. The tranquillity seemed unnatural. The teacher was friendly and spoke quietly. The boys and he were on familiar terms; even a gently humorous remark was not unacceptable on either side, a state of things that simply could not have happened at the other school. But a very striking thing was that the Head never came into the room. I wondered why.

Through our slightly built, bespectacled young teacher came new pleasures in learning. There was a science room complete with bottles and flasks and test-tubes that we could use, but alas, the pleasure was never realized. The master had newly graduated in science and he left us for a post at a Grammar School.

54

His place was taken by a young man about to go up to university and the friendly atmosphere was maintained. In those short weeks we found it exciting to have a teacher only a few years older than ourselves, young enough to be still a boy. The chief gain from this period was to be free from mass instruction and to work individually, with the teacher approachable all the time. Informality was the rule.

To lose him was another misfortune. A few weeks later came a great surprise. For some reason I shall never understand he sent me a single volume of "The Complete Works of William Shakespeare," a volume I have been happy to preserve through all the years.

If life at the new school could have preserved the joys of those first weeks, it would have been a place to revel in. One person, however, regarded the scene with a different eye — the Head. He towered over every person and object in the school. Remarkably erect for his age, with hair, moustache and beard of greenish-grey and a rose-red mottled face, he strode the floor as his kingdom. When he walked, the boards creaked. When he barked, everything trembled. His clothes sagged about him. His overcoat had once been navy blue. Sun, rain and the years had transformed it to bottle-green, his favourite colour.

It soon became obvious he did not approve of the methods used in the small room, or even of the people there. Theirs was not the technique of learning that he had known for so long. This nonsense of moving about the room, working on one's own, smilingly consulting the teacher about one's problem, had to cease. He had bided his time and now the hour had come. Out from the privacy of the secluded room we were thrust and bundled unceremoniously into the big room.

"Now we shall see what work is," he bawled, while in the right side pocket of his jacket, his hand toyed malevolently with his ever-present weapon, a chair-leg. No refinement of a cane for him. Wherever he was, the chair leg was a hidden symbol of vengeance. It was used to crack a joke, too; the greatest wonder was it never cracked a skull.

So the battle of life and for survival was resumed.

How we worked! He drove us as fiercely as ever captives were driven through the wilderness. It was not unknown for his huge boot to urge into action the slothful or unsuspecting boy who, while working out sums on his slate, standing out of class on the floor, failed to be vigilant enough to safeguard his posterior from attack from behind. On such occasions we heard a sudden, violent crash as the victim collided with the wall.

In oral lessons two classes crowded into the long desks of one class. Squeezed together, we had little or no room to move hands or arms, so our legs sought relief in kicking that part of the anatomy that protruded from the seats in front. The first row, sadly, had no one to kick.

Enter the Head. Looking over this mass of humanity he spotted his victim – at the end of a row. He strode along to the target area - the "target" as yet unaware that he had been selected – as the teacher continued to do his duty. Within three feet of the victim he yelled his name and with a swift sweep of the chair leg crashed it onto the head or shoulder of the victim. But having once learned, the victim acted with incredible speed. As the blow descended, he thrust himself with superhuman force against the long line of sitting human flesh. Less prepared than he, in one brief moment they slid along the seat; those at the other end collapsed on the floor like an avalanche. For this unseemly disturbance and chaos, those who had fallen became recipients of the chair leg, and the original target was forgotten. We preserved our sanity by laughing about it. I think he laughed too.

Often in mid-morning he would call a boy to come to him, and, holding out money in one hand, he would say, "Go and get me The Telegraph." Seeing his other hand in a certain pocket the boy edged cautiously forward to near striking distance, but before the weapon could finish its flight, he had grabbed the money and was in full retreat.

For another, very different request he became a different man. Gone the awesome manner and voice, now a low, confidential whisper.

"Herbert." "Sir". "Go down to the Park Hotel and ask them to give you my walking-stick. And don't forget to say 'Thank you'."

The Park was his favourite evening resort. He regularly forgot to take the stick home but usually managed to get there without it. Just once he failed, being taken instead to hospital, with both legs fractured.

I have always marvelled that this man never tired of his job or of us. Standard Seven was ever in his thoughts. Our seclusion in the far room meant there was much to atone for, and he was determined we should pay for that in full.

When four o'clock arrived and the end of the day, we stood for prayers. The Benediction had not yet died away, the second syllable of the Amen still echoing in the lofty room, when he bellowed forth, "Standard Seven, SIT." Inwardly we groaned, until after the first few days we realized that this was going to be a permanent addition to our school day. Overtime every day but Friday. He must have conceded that social pressures on Friday were too strong to destroy.

SIT! And we sat, enviously watching the long line of those passing out to freedom, half-glancing at us, fearing to glance wholly lest they might be commanded to join us, smiling the glad smile of those "who are not as other men." Waiting was misery.

Then broke forth all the fury of one possessed by the demon of English Grammar, fascinated with the urge to parse and analyse – nouns with first, second or third person; number singular or plural; gender masculine or feminine or neuter; case nominative; objective or possessive – or anything else there might be. Every part of speech we knew in detail. And the most involved extracts from William Shakespeare and other guilty people were carefully selected for our everlasting confusion, with principal sentences and subordinate clauses and clauses of other and varying description (and sometimes defying description).

Quite often that hour began in a subdued tone. There was a tension – as if the Headmaster was inwardly gauging the lengths to which he might go in this fiendish war – but it was only to let the Amen die wholly away. Then the storm broke. There were never gentle summer gales; the thunder crashed and the lightning flashed. Not even for overtime could the stick be withdrawn. There must have been some sad frustration in his life, and he took it out on us. But in this way I was introduced to great passages of English literature that took an hour to analyse and parse. Later at the Grammar School the treatment of English Grammar was very much an anti–climax.

As the colliery buzzer blew five o'clock, we left the school. The boys on the belts would just be finishing too. We worked as hard as they.

In the wide open space of the playground, smoothly asphalted, much larger than at the last school, we could tear round in freedom. As long as we ran there was pleasure. If we indulged in ball games, there were always problems. Along the north side of the yard ran a stone wall only three feet high, separating our area from the garden of the house next to the school. The garden was several feet below the playground. It was easy to jump into the garden but difficult to climb out.

With the first shouts of schoolboys let out into the sunshine and fresh air, the lady of the house also emerged to take the air. Concealing herself among the shrubs and bushes she waited and watched, her dog beside her. This was her lone, fiendish pleasure. We made every effort to keep the ball low, passing it along the ground as much as possible, but, inevitably, the opportunity for a hard drive presented itself. Then, sad to relate, the ball rose high, described a lovely parabola over the yard and descended all too swiftly into the forbidden garden.

There were, however, experts to deal with this situation; no sooner was the fateful flight of the ball observed than Gordon, with equal swiftness, leaped the wall to follow the ball and rescue it for our further enjoyment. He had to contend with the dog, however, while the lady sought the ball. If she found it first, Gordon beat his retreat, the dog doing his best to spoil his trousers–seat as he scrambled up the wall. Then we gazed across in dumb defeat, as she revealed the knife she was carrying and slashed the ball with it. She did not always win though, and loud cheers would greet the safe return of our champion. Whenever the dog was seen away from the house, its unpopularity was demonstrated in several ways. So the war went on, within and without the fortress. We learned to make the best of both worlds.

Quite unexpectedly something happened which marked the first important change in my life. One day, before afternoon session, I heard my name ring out in those stentorian tones that chilled the blood. I stood stock–still. My mind raced furiously through the events of the last few hours and my conscience burned. What had I done to incur this great wrath? I turned to look at the towering figure. His right hand was not in its customary pocket. I waited.

"Come here," he called in yet unyielding voice.

I walked towards him. He turned, and I followed him to one of the long desks near his own.

"Sit there," he said. "Here's a good pen. Now I want you to fill in this form." He produced a printed foolscap sheet of paper with headings in bold capitals; below them and at the side, in smaller print were words like 'name, address, date of birth, father's name' and so on. Under his direction the entries were made He picked up the sheet, folded it and placed it in a long envelope already addressed and stamped. "Now run up to the post-box and post it," he said, "and tell your father you are going to sit an examination."

It was incomprehensible. Even though obviously interested in me, having specially chosen me to sit the examination for a County Scholarship, he could scarcely unbend. The exam was not mentioned again until the day I was told where to go and at what time.

(That same week I was transferred to yet another school. Pressure on accommodation had now affected our school, and this was met by transferring the top classes from both boys' and girls' departments to form a new mixed school called a Higher Grade School, housed in a church hall. Thus in less than twelve months I was a pupil in three different schools, with different teachers and different conditions.)

I sat the examination, for a County award, and a few weeks later I sat another for a scholarship at the local Grammar School. In spite of the changes I had experienced, I had reason to be grateful for the separate and distinctive contributions each had made to my education.

The end of the summer term came with excitement such as had not been known in the family. It was Tuesday evening, and with other boys I was playing cricket on the Green – two wooden boards for wickets supported at the rear with half bricks, the stumps chalked in white on the board – when in the distance I spied my sister Ada, obviously looking for me. When she caught my eye, she waved to me to come, and the gesture was an urgent one.

"You've passed," she called. The postman had just delivered the letter on his evening round. The whole family was excited. I was offered a scholarship for one year, renewable for a second "in the event of satisfactory progress". This was through the second exam I had sat. Next day father sent off a letter of acceptance.

The following Saturday began with the excitement of the Miners' Gala. Everyone was up early that morning and before eight o'clock folk were thronging the street down which would march the local colliery contingent, headed by the brass band, lodge officials and others with the richly decorated silk banner which sent a thrill like no other through the heart of every miner. This was their banner and this was pride of life. As the company marched past to the stirring music of the band, the postman handed father a foolscap envelope. The excitement over, we went indoors. Now we could have breakfast.

"You've passed again," he exclaimed. The letter brought news of the award of a County Scholarship tenable at Bishop Auckland Grammar School, renewable for four years. It was the most fortunate predicament that one could be in. The choice was not mine to make, though. Father consulted the Heads who had shared in this success and on their advice the first acceptance was withdrawn with the Head's permission and the second offer taken up because it made possible not merely two, but four years' education at a Grammar School.

I marvel at the ease with which my parents made their decision. The economic position of the family was still insecure. There were three sisters at home older than myself, each bringing in a few shillings a week, there were also at school two younger brothers and three young sisters. Eleven in the household to feed and clothe, and here was I being committed to four years at a Grammar School. At the end of that time I would be seventeen years old.

In such a community at that time you normally became a wage-earner at fourteen, those with Labour Certificates at twelve. In every family the few shillings a week which young people could bring in made the difference between living and 'scraping'. To walk along the street when fifteen or sixteen not having as yet contributed anything to the family pool - for pool it was - was to incur unfavourable comments in some quarters. I remember how, when I was nearly sixteen, mother asked me to do some shopping for her at a grocer's shop near by. The shop was filled with waiting women. I stood among them for my turn.

"When are you going to start work, boy?" the shopkeeper suddenly called to me across the waiting crowd. It stunned me. I shall never forget his scornful tone. To be asked such a question and in such a way and in such a place appalled me. It seemed that I was guilty of some crime.

I stood silent, ignoring the question. To myself I said, "You dreadful person. My father has never said that to me." When my turn came I asked for as few things as possible. I wanted to get out. I was served without comment but could never be persuaded to enter that shop again.

It had still not yet been realized that education was worth having for such families as ours or for such a community, even. There were few opportunities: my County award was the only one within a radius of several miles; moreover, there were no maintenance grants whatsoever. Only those who knew at first hand the harsh struggle for a bare living, year in and year out, could appreciate why, even if there had been more prospects, it was difficult for parents to sacrifice. Their lives were already sacrificial. But because my parents saw beyond their immediate needs, I was given my opportunity. No man has greater cause for gratitude to his parents than I.

CB&O

GRAMMAR SCHOOL

On a September morning in 1906 I boarded the train for my first journey to the Grammar School in Bishop Auckland. Some fee-payers from the town travelled by the same train, but as a new boy I was alone. In the school I joined the other beginners standing uncertainly around, awed by the strange surroundings and an inward loneliness. Most of the boys were entering under a teacher—candidate scheme and were older than myself. The obvious question to ask each other was, "Where do you live?" We were a very mixed crowd from villages and small towns within a radius of about twelve miles, but we faced cheerfully the prospect of a long day —in my case from 8.30 a.m. to 6.30 p.m. and homework to do after that.

Even on that first day no time was wasted. After new books were distributed we plunged into lessons. The building was small and compact. From the staff room the masters could reach any classroom within seconds. They swung into a lesson as soon as the bell stopped and swung out again as soon as it signalled the end. So we learned what was meant by good timekeeping. Generally the master moved; classes remained, except for lessons in the Labs. This early stimulus was most valuable. We were kept on our toes, and for the first time in my life I realized the pleasure of having to think quickly, to think ahead, with thirty other like—minded boys doing the same.

We soon discovered that with one particular master there could be a measure of discreet relaxation. Generally he resorted to a boy's desk at the rear of the class and from that point directed operations quite dispassionately. Maybe he was seeing through us; I never knew. Occasionally he had the startling idea of resorting to the blackboard at the front to illustrate some point — quite usefully as it turned out — but he seemed out of place there and inevitably retreated to the obscurity of the rear as soon as possible. It was sometimes confusing to be directed from the rear and we learned to judge by sound and not by sight. When afternoon school ended, he was the first to dash out, and when we emerged he could be seen far down the road, his short, brisk step taking him, almost as a matter of urgency, into the country with the exhilaration of a man freed from long bondage.

The school had been a private foundation supported by private pupils, children of tradesmen and professional people. The extension of Secondary Education resulted in the school opening its doors to pupils selected by the Local Authority. In subsequent years the number of pupils entering with scholarships increased considerably. My own entry was at a time when one became aware that something of past glory was being tenaciously held against the invasion of a different order. But we were there to be educated and to enjoy the process as much as we could. Compared with our teachers in the elementary schools, who pursued us all the day and watched us with eagle eye at every turn, our new masters were quite indifferent to our person. They were there to teach a subject, and we were there to take it.

When the long shadow of the maths master fell upon our domain, the temperature fell too. With him there was no nonsense; we worked, relentlessly .... Algebra, Euclid, Trigonometry. The stuff had to be known. He had performed his act. Ours was to learn, and - yes, to reason why, and then to tell him so. He would not accept defeat.

"One o'clock then." Those words were dreaded. That was the penalty of failure, failure to learn a proposition and to demonstrate it on the blackboard to the whole form without error. Those three words were the knell of an abbreviated lunchtime.

At one o'clock we returned to the room. He was already there. We had sacrificed the playing-field. He had sacrificed too - but not his pipe. He would demand, he would urge and press with frigid insistence, he would stride to and fro talking all the while, but he never ceased to puff. It was pleasant to watch the blue smoke curl and dissolve into the air. Other mists were dissolving too.

Latin and French were treated with similar thoroughness, but the masters preferred not to surrender their personal pleasures for our discomfort. It was in the labs that we experienced the thrills of new subjects like Chemistry and Physics, one pleasurable, the other not so.

In the middle of the second year we were informed that we would sit a University Local Examination at the end of the year. There was no attempt to whip us into a frenzy, no piling on the pressure, no working of old examination papers, no attempts at predicting the questions we were certain to get this time. My first sight of such a paper was when I sat at my desk in the examinations room in the shadow of Durham Cathedral and found a white octavo sheet placed thereon for my delectation. The end section, I read, was to be worked if a distinction was desired. We had not been told that distinctions could be collected. (Unfortunately my own school was not a centre for the exam. Each morning I left home at a quarter to eight and returned at seven in the evening, with lunch and tea to get where I could. By the end of the week the experience proved quite exhausting.)

After the school holiday there was a fair lack of interest in the results, which had already been announced in the local newspapers. Indeed, some of the boys had already left to take up employment on reaching fifteen. But no inquest was held or comments made. We were merely told the next exam would be at the end of the third year. So, among other features of a repetitive scene, we continued our closer acquaintance with "Julius Caesar" for a second year.

At sixteen I became a pupil-teacher. Under the new arrangements for this course half the time was spent at the Grammar School in preparation for an examination by the Board of Education at the end of the course. The other half was passed in an Elementary School, where one was expected to observe the methods of the experienced teachers and also acquire some experience of actual teaching.

Each week it was my task to prepare one special lesson, known as a "Criticism Lesson", to be given in the presence of the Head and/or the class teacher, who then wrote comments on it in a special book.

My first "Crit Lesson" was scarcely believable. The subject allotted to me was "Leaves". The Head had become greatly interested in Nature Study as a school subject, but at no point in my school life had I learnt anything in a systematic way about living things. (Biology had not then come into its own.) In my first week in the school there had been no chance to see what had been done before, but I collected specimens, drew sketches and went into battle with high-spirited nine-year old boys. And my half-hour lesson finished in five minutes. The boys knew more about it than I, for they had heard it all before! They were ready to tell me what I was about to deal with even before I could begin. I was utterly defeated. The Head, however, gallantly came to the rescue, realizing the impossibility of teaching the same thing twice, especially as he had taught it the first time!

This experience was thus a mixture of slow learning, steady acquisition of some teaching skill, a discernment of standards about which I would have to make my own decisions - and utter boredom. Much of the time would have been more profitably spent in higher academic studies at the Grammar School.

A consoling feature of the new status, however, was that it was salaried service. In the first year, aged sixteen, I was paid ten pounds per annum and each month I had to sign on the dotted line of the pay sheet to show that I had received the sum of sixteen shillings and eight pence. In the second year the amount was fifteen pounds. Four shillings a week! This was the encouragement to young people to give their lives to the cause of education, which, it was now proclaimed, was so essential for national progress. It was also an encouragement to parents who could not afford to give their children to this service; though four shillings a week did not make much real difference.

Before returning to the Grammar School for the next exam hurdle, I decided to take the Matriculation Examination of London University in the hope that somewhere along the line I would take a degree. But the Grammar School made no provision for this and I was left to my own devices to plan out the additional work required for the exam over and above school requirements. Except for the Head no other member of the staff showed interest.

My biggest thrill was when one of my form mates startled me by saying that he too would sit the exam, merely to keep me company. It was a most sacrificial gesture. He had not prepared as I had done for months past, but in one wonderful week of the Christmas holidays he kept me company in the exam room. Apart from the time in the examination room we enjoyed ourselves, in spite of snow on one day, which nearly made havoc of everything. I was very sorry when his name was missing from the Pass List, as I was when a few years later he was again 'missing' - in the course of the First World War.

In concentrating on the requirements of Matriculation I had neglected Geography, which I had not selected for that examination, and I appalled my Geography master with a mark not much above zero. With Matriculation out of the way I had then a clear eight weeks to retrieve the position. As an aid I took a correspondence course in the subject for two months, and, it goes without saying, I worked hard. When the results of the examination were announced, one of two distinctions I had gained was in Geography and it was the only one from the Form. I have often wondered what the master of the back seat thought about that success gained for his subject.

During the five years I spent at the Grammar School important changes took place. The number of fee—payers diminished appreciably: the great proportion of admissions came from County awards of various kinds, and the greater the predominance of the proletariat, the less distinctive became the special occasions of the year such as Speech Day and Sports Day. They were still observed but the brightness of the glory departed.

A striking feature of school life was the lack of personal interest shown in pupils. No master ever asked about our hopes or ambitions for a career. Most of us were earmarked for teaching, but all the information we obtained about seeking admission to college was gleaned from boys who knew someone already there. There was no advisory service and, from the lack of reference to University, it was assumed there was not the slightest hope for any of us to go there.

Our mid—day sandwiches were eaten more or less as we chose, often sitting at our own desk in the form-room. We talked as we ate then vanished into the field or the woods or the town. There were no school societies, no evening clubs; we came and went. For three years some of us had to wait till nearly six o'clock for a train home in a dimly lit room where work was not possible. It seemed that no one thought the school might have a social contribution to offer.

The stress on the purely academic nature of our education was seen in the almost complete disregard for art, music and physical education. The latter was non-existent, even as 'drill'. Occasionally we might be released from a lesson and told to go and kick a ball around on the field. There was no gymnasium, nor any place where organized exercises might take place. Drawing was taken by a visiting master one day a week, during which he visited all classes taking the subject.

'Music' was really community singing, with the whole school assembled on the ground floor, a partition drawn back to form one room out of two. The available seats were shared by the younger pupils, the older standing at the rear or in the distant corners, where they could pursue their own non-musical interests.

The visiting master sat at the piano. He was a distinguished musician, a church organist, *and* choirmaster, which made little impression on most of us, whose voices at that time were not very musical. He invited us so pleasantly to go forth to war with the minstrel boy, or to bemoan the fact that Robin was not where he should be, or to enquire where our Highland laddie had gone.

Most of us were not interested in these wandering creatures and there were even versions of some of those lyrics that were not for publication. The juniors nearest the piano sang lustily and heartily with the sweet treble that earned them the honour of representing the musical life of the school on Prize Day. The master was quite a delightful person. He always seemed to enjoy that half–hour immensely. We, too, could smile with him when the end came.

I have always appreciated the academic training I received, though the pupil-teacher course was insufficiently exacting. Other features of school are scored deep in my mind. In the first decade of the twentieth century, when children from working-class homes were beginning to attend Grammar Schools, there was a slowness to realize the significance of the change, and an air of tolerance, unwilling at times, towards this "invasion" of the ancient foundation.

In our first week at school one of the masters informed us that he was responsible for the provision of games equipment, and in order to enable the school to purchase football and cricket gear, each boy was expected to pay half-a-crown for the football season and another for cricket in the summer term.

Half-a-crown! This was 1906. Most of us had never handled such a sum, except for shopping. It was a fortune. The silence that followed this announcement was eloquent. This was something not to talk about, and we looked at each other, dumb and afraid.

I made the request of my father, my breath quickening as I spoke; after a strained pause the half-crown changed hands. I paid it over, as did most ... but not all.

For these Monday morning became misery Monday. It brought a monologue, which, for brevity, intensity and shared suffering is vivid in recollection. It unnerved us. It made us angry. We knew the meaning of the silence. A quiet, decent lad, dumb in his torture and suffering, sensitive in his silence, afraid to speak the sad truth that we all knew. His father's wage was less than a pound a week. Half-a-crown out of that was a tidy sum.

And that master — far removed from the life of people rejoicing in the selection of their boy for a Grammar School education — did not, could not or would not see that some just had no money to pay for games. Things began to dawn on us. It was true what we had been told: books were provided free; we had free passes for railway travel; everything was free. Except sport. To boys who had been thrilled at the prospect of learning Latin and French, Mathematics, Physics and Chemistry, the realization of this seared the soul.

Some time later another incident occurred. At the close of a lesson when a master had outraged all good sense by the way he spoke, the long-suffering form hissed him as he left. Swinging round, he stared in scornful silence, then commanded, "One o'clock, all of you."

At one o'clock the Form lined up in the Lab, a floorboard prescribing the straight line desired. Then, as if in preparing for those inspection parades that were to become so familiar in a few short years to all of us, the inquisition commenced.

"And where do you live?" "Mount Pleasant, sir." "And what is your father?" "Colliery engineer, sir." "Ummmmmm. Well, we can't expect anything better from you."

And so it continued, from one end of the line to the other. The same remorseless cruelty, to make us aware that folk living on a low social level could never behave otherwise than on a low level. This incivility of the master was a new force difficult to counter. Against this sort of unfeeling disparagement we had no weapon. It left us speechless but rebellious.

For my academic success I have been grateful for the contribution of the Grammar School. Its attitude to pupils, though, indicates that while it programmed a curriculum in preparation for examinations for entry to the teaching profession, it showed little awareness of any social contribution it could make to our development.

Since that time one of the most outstanding changes has been the recognition of the individuality of young people. To meet young folk today from the Sixth Forms of Grammar Schools is to be impressed with their quality as individuals whose cultural life is richer than in preceding generations. The schools alone have not effected this, but the part played by teachers and administrators has been appreciable.

CB80

THE TRIP

In a world of so many new, often bewildering, sensations we still found great pleasure in the anticipation and enjoyment of experiences that we had not yet outgrown. One of these was the annual Sunday School excursion ... known as "The Trip".

We always went on The Trip, even in our teens; this was the annual excursion to the seaside organized by the Sunday Schools of the town. A week's holiday by the sea was out of the question for families like ours, so we all went on the Sunday School Trip. It was our only opportunity in the year. The train fare was tenpence for children, half of this paid by the Sunday School. Who would refuse the chance of a long day by the sea for fivepence? Whole families went, except for the fathers, who would have had to lose a shift, and that was rather too expensive, so the mothers did their best to make the outing a memorable one.

The day before the trip mother spent much time making pies and cakes to feed the family, and packing them so that the bags had only to be lifted from the table for us boys to carry them to the railway station about a mile away.

There hundreds of parents and children waited excitedly for the arrival of the special train that would take us direct to the seaside. The journey was excitement in itself. There would usually be ten of us to a compartment, and if the family managed to get one to itself, then mother knew where we all were. As journey's end approached, we would crowd to the windows on the side where the sea was, and at first sight of the blue water a cry of "The Sea, The Sea!" rose from many throats, from thrilling whisper to high-sounding shrieks of joy.

With the release of everyone from the station precincts the struggle began to maintain control against the mounting excitement. Which was the shortest way to the sands? In this the North-East excels; instead of beaches with shingle and pebbles that impede movement, making walking or even turning over difficult, we have glorious, golden, clean sand, where on a sunny summer's day you can lie and laze in warmth and ease without thought of pebbly discomfort. Here is glistening sand that runs through the fingers; sand that children might cascade from small buckets on father's tummy as he reclines full length in the hole he has dug for them; sand where children and grown-ups can play at cricket, summer football and racing, and where the children enjoy the frustrating walk of a donkey-ride.

The level sands gave joy to young children - but to older ones the level town, with its long straight roads, offered another thrill that they talked about in the train. "Are you going to get a bike out?"

For sixpence they hired a cycle, a real bicycle, for one hour. Back home a few of them basked in the proud ownership of what was described as a "boneshaker", a description that usually was literally true, awkward to steer, with tyres of solid rubber (often worn to the rim), an unsprung seat, a heavy frame - a machine to rattle the bones indeed, and even to cripple one for life. To roll round the town as proud owner of a "real" flying steed, even for only one hour, would make the day memorable.

Before the trippers had reached the sands they were overtaken by the first of the mounted horde who, heads down, pretended they were scorching the road to the sea. It was essentially an individual enterprise, but after the first flush of excitement, they raced in pairs. Then, with the invigorating air of the sea stirring them to new enterprise, they formed a small club and moved off in grand style, a dozen or more, side by side, wheel to wheel, heads down and spirits high. Along the promenade, past the pier, on towards the sand hills, inland by the golf course, back by the cemetery, the Railway Station and High Street, to the finishing post by the pier. Dismounting, they stood beside their machines, proud veterans of the road, one hand resting on the saddle, the other mopping the brow or lightly touching the handlebars, talking of what to do next. The greatest need was for pop and ice cream and in these they indulged freely. After all, they had been saving all the year, and it was to spend on a day like this.

The next great adventure was to bathe in the sea. A few yards from the water was a line of bathing vans, wooden huts on wheels, in which you removed your clothes and put on the bathing costume hired for fourpence. A towel cost threepence and the charge for using the van was fourpence. We entered the landward side by ascending wooden steps, and while we were preparing for the water, the owner harnessed a horse to the seaward side, and within a few seconds the van stood in the sea at a depth suitable for our exploits. The horse was withdrawn and we gazed with mingled fear and joy at the prospect, so rare to us in our lives. With three or four of us undressing in one van there was a great deal of fun, exceeded only by the cold douche in the sea. None of us could swim (a rare accomplishment at that time) but that we had tasted the brine was something more to sing about as we returned.

Cycles, sands and sea, simple pleasures on one great day in the year. But another remained— to see that one was spent-up!

Returning to the station I found myself looking in the window of a bookshop. There, for sixpence, was a new series of books, some with titles I had not heard before. I went inside.

"I can get two of those with my last shilling," I thought. And I did. I bought "Oliver Twist" by Charles Dickens and "The Last of the Mohicans" by Fennimore Cooper. Over the years I have made several attempts to read the latter but it remains unfinished even now.

I started to read "Oliver Twist" in the train and was captivated by it. For me no other person in that compartment existed; I was transported. It was the first real book that I had bought and it is still a landmark in my realm of books. I could think of nothing else. I would have read it in bed if I could and as I went off to school next morning "Oliver Twist" was in my bag, to read in the train.

When the Chief came in to take us for French, he spotted me. "You had the day off yesterday, didn't you?" "Yes, sir," I replied. "I was at the seaside."

"At the Dog Show?" came the bruising question. I ached with anger. Dog Show? I had never heard of a dog show; I did not know what one was. It sounded dreadful though. Was it so disreputable to be interested in dogs? He really should have known better. He must have known better. But with the condescending snobbery of the ancient foundation this could not be resisted.

"No, sir," I replied, miserable. "It was the Sunday School trip."

What I really wanted to say, and I wanted to shout it so that the earth could hear, and I wanted him to share my joy, was— "No, sir, not the Dog Show. I DISCOVERED OLIVER TWIST."

⋐⋑

CHAPEL

Chapel was the one place, apart from home, where an important part of our young lives was spent. It was a place that had a stabilizing influence and was the source of most of our childhood joys, even of some sorrows.

Many miners and their families were religious, in the sense that they went regularly to church and chapel. Lying in on Sunday mornings to make up sleep lost in the week, they turned out for evening service, and large congregations were the rule. That is not to say that morning service was neglected. Some went to both. And over the mantelpiece in many a house hung a coloured card, beautifully lettered, announcing from the central place in the home -

CHRIST IS THE HEAD OF THIS HOUSE,
THE UNSEEN GUEST AT EVERY MEAL,
THE UNSEEN LISTENER TO EVERY CONVERSATION.

The chapel was our second home. Its activities were the chief topic of conversation - the Minister, the Sunday School Superintendent, the teachers, the Choir, the Anniversary, the concerts and the socials. Church and chapel were community centres. There was no pretension to lofty cultural activities, but in debating societies and literary clubs the more intelligent men in the community found an outlet. With little formal schooling, these men had educated themselves; their knowledge of literature, history and philosophy would have put to shame many today who claim to be educated. In these meetings they practised the art of public speaking, and their ability to express themselves clearly and succinctly (to the amazement of many listeners) marked In such meetings were nurtured leaders of trades unions, often with experience of preaching that religious conviction led them to undertake. (Women, however, had not reached the stage where they were expected to show interest or play a part in such matters; theirs was a full-time job, to stay at home and look after the family.

In times when society in general was static, the little chapel had a secluded kind of existence. When things changed, they changed slowly. At the chapel they changed even more slowly. "The things that cannot be shaken" was taken all too literally by those who regarded themselves as guardians of the spiritual and moral condition of the flock. In spite of earthquakes and scientific advances, irrespective of evolutionists and archaeologists, they could not be shaken. This presented a difficulty for those who understood something of the revolution in thought that had come in with the century.

The chapel was dominated in its organization and administration by laymen. At some periods a full-time minister was invited to serve the church, but the government of the church proceeded through its meeting of church members, where any member was permitted to speak and where decisions were taken by a vote of the members. An elected body of deacons served as spiritual leaders and advisers.

To be nurtured in this spiritual democracy affected my life in every aspect. The theory was excellent; the members were responsible for the life and progress of the church. In practice, however, not all were able or willing to accept this duty, which was a very serious commitment.

The laymen took great pride in running the church. So long as they remembered they were serving God, and not merely running an institution that was their own personal property and pride, they could be instruments of great purpose. In my boyhood the leaders had a limited intellectual background, but their guiding faith was a strong conviction based on their interpretation of the Bible, particularly the New Testament (though they found the Old Testament more congenial to their type of preaching). They were not, as a rule, prepared to discuss matters of faith but rested confidently on *their* interpretation of the Scriptures. If rumour were abroad that some scholar or divine had expressed a new interpretation of an old doctrine, he was decisively dismissed. What the Bible said could not be changed. That meant that what they said, the Bible said! The scholar, generally, was suspect, since he might well deprive them of their most treasured possession.

So, as a youth in my teens, still being educated, I was regarded by some as suspect, "growing away from it."

In fairness to the oldest members it must be remembered that they were largely self-educated. Some had learned to read in the early days of Sunday Schools, where illiterate working-men found the gates of paradise opening slightly for them, and by dint of effort they opened them wider, with the Bible as their book. It was then much less the Book for scholarly study than we know now. So there were no problems.

The two chief figures in the church were strangely complementary; one of limited outlook, impetuous in action and speech, and in kindness too; the other thoughtful, balanced in every way, generous too, even to other men's faults. To the first the young ladies were attracted, to the second the men were drawn.

It was not, however, intellect that ruled. These folk imposed on themselves a way of life in which everything was subordinate to what they regarded as the Christian way of life, inspired by the faith they held. The congregation consisted almost entirely of working people, miners, and one or two who had ventured into business or independent occupations. When social differences appeared, the community lost something of the element that had early bound it together. They were happiest with a single- stratum society, but their concept of spiritual democracy did not convict them of any inconsistency.

Sunday School was a happy place. Boys and girls and young people who thronged there every Sunday afternoon came just because it was so, and it had moreover no competition from secular attractions in those days. Even though many of those youngsters had ceased to attend church by the time they were grown up, it influenced the lives of many more of them than it is usually given credit for.

For boys, the highest ambition was to be admitted at the age of fourteen to the young men's Bible Class, among the men, the eldest of whom - at about forty - was described as "the ancient of days." These older men comported themselves with stolid detachment, proud of the loyalty that still took them there, oozing the authority that the years gave them and that their humble daily work denied them. They would all claim upright living and in their austerity they had great pride.

It was their solemn responsibility to see that the fourteen-year-olds, newly entered each summer, grew into their great tradition, which they counted above all else. The Leader dominated by his presence, a spirit well poised and a mind well stored, a determination to seek after truth, and a habit of speaking only when necessary. If there were a fault, it lay in too great a tolerance.

To develop a social life of their own became their proud ambition. They spent evenings in each other's homes, practising for a Concert Party that toured the district, in black-and-white striped minstrel costumes, entertaining with items of music, drama and humour. They packed the halls, giving folk what they loved - an evening of happy laughter, served up by men they knew. In the summer they spent a week at a camp in the country, all the equipment being purchased from class funds. From these activities they derived much pleasure and they were proud that the chapel was their home. My own pre-occupation with Grammar School and homework compelled me to refrain from participation. To men who daily engaged in the exertions of coal-getting, this form of relaxation, promoted by themselves when no other opportunities existed, was a commendable enterprise.

They failed, however, to appreciate that there was another world in which values were different. They had not known the excitement of intellectual quest. They read the Bible round the class, a verse at a time, as had been done since anyone could remember, but they never read a book about the Bible or the things that men believe. They never knew such books existed, and even if they did, they deemed them not for the likes of them. So they never asked any questions. There were none to ask. And he who found he could frame a question might feel suddenly isolated in the silence that descended.

All except one. For his turn each week the silent ones looked on. He looked as if he could move mountains. He might have led revolutions but he contented himself to speak the Word. When he opened his mouth others might tremble. He quoted from someone called George Bernard Shaw, who wrote plays; a fellow called Blatchford, a Socialist; and a novelist named Hardy. And there were other names that were from a world unknown even to the minister. He made it exciting. And he even had something to say once about a god called Mithras and bulls and blood. When he talked like this, they wondered why he was there at all, with his flowing tongue and his tremendous energy.

In the first stage of his exposition he was exciting. In the second, asking his question, he shocked some of them. And in the third, answering tirelessly, with all the assurance of omniscience, the question that no one cared about at all, the gradually decreasing interest showed itself in boredom that was felt as well as seen.

But they tolerated him. He was one of them. He lived in the same street, worked at the same pit. But how he got those ideas baffled them. He had read and found a world that was never theirs.

One afternoon came another surprise. Someone asked a question, one of the newcomers, who were expected to be seen and not heard.

The address had been about the obligation of the Christian to separate himself from the world.

"Why do you say that a Christian should not attend the theatre?"

This newcomer had never been to a theatre but was reading Shakespeare's Plays, and Shakespeare was meant to be acted, in a live place, and by great actors and actresses. Why was it wrong to go where one could see and hear them? Why?

In the strained silence someone shuffled in his seat. Why ask this? He should know the answer. They did. It was a familiar theme in the life of churches. An eager youth who wished to know how to meet situations that they and their like had not had to confront, misunderstood by those belonging to a one-stratum society that expected only unquestioning conformity who had not thought about the problem, was becoming isolated. This was the place to enquire; he hoped the answer would be helpful.

The answer was a perfectly sincere expression of what the speaker thought about the small town theatre and its visiting players.

"The theatre is the work of the devil. These women who daily walk the streets of the town in their feathered finery, dyed hair and painted faces, are walking Jezebels, women on whom God might have mercy. And the men? They aid and abet the women in their evil ways. How can a Christian attend such a place to watch such people?

"It is an evil place. Stay away from it. Seek not temptation. To go signifies your approval. You would be no better than they."

It was as simple as that. But it was not the answer to the question. It expressed the outlook that characterized the small town and the small church of that day. It was severe in judgement, sweeping and condemnatory. And it confused the issue. It was not one of the character and probity of the players, but whether the Christian could legitimately enjoy the art of the theatre.

Here issues were thought to be clear-cut, so answers could be decisive. A new commandment had appeared. "Thou shalt do as I tell thee." One should not think so much.

And as men left their places for the open air, they looked at each other in silence, but their eyes were eloquent with concern. On one thing they were certainly agreed; they had no need to say it aloud. That people might be changed by reading or by education, which was different from mere school, scarcely dawned on them. Defensively they erected a barrier against anything they did not understand, that placed them at a disadvantage. If books were mentioned for the stimulus of their ideas, silence descended. Poetry was limited to the type of recitation that moved a homely audience to laughter or to tears. Music? One could gossip freely during a piano solo, it wasn't something to listen to really. That new tastes were forming, new intellectual and emotional experiences being enjoyed could not be appreciated. They did not like folk who were different. They were proud of their conformity.

In the follies of teenagers salvation was found. We ridiculed the overlordship of elders who had no sympathy with the new generation and we excused their irrational and uncharitable actions. But there came a point when our youthful enthusiasm and idealism become severely strained by this protracted lack of comprehension of our point of view.

Miraculously a young minister came on the scene who soon interested himself in one Grammar School boy longing for understanding. That was the point at which my life became dedicated to the cause of education and to the service of the Church.

As leader of the Bible Class this young minister brought a new and lively mind to the task. Old ideas were examined, surprising some and bringing to others the light that they had long been waiting for. Strikingly he sought to cultivate a spirit of tolerance. There was no monopoly of truth; Jesus had urged men to love one another, regardless of colour, race and creed, but it also meant doing it in spite of difference of opinions and experience. The bigotry of some church folk exceeded their charity. Men had to live by the truths to which their minds had given acceptance. And they learned to ask questions and to listen to the genuine desire of others to know about things that were puzzling them.

Attracted by the new minister came Tom, a young man already interested in preaching, gifted with striking eloquence and power of study - quite a revelation in a man who worked daily as a labourer. Then there was 'Gip', who earned the reputation of the clown in the concert party, and whose lack of intellectual power was made up for by a great friendliness and capacity for sympathy. Lastly there was Arthur, slower to think and speak, who found study more difficult than the rest. His elder brother had already entered the ministry.

Through these newcomers a more stimulating element distinguished the meetings, and horizons broadened.

Before Tom left for College he used to play outside-left with us on the football team. As in his thinking, he knew where the goal was.

Arthur, Gip and I, with the minister as our coach, prepared ourselves for the national examination for lay preachers, after which both Arthur and Gip proceeded to a London college to train for the ministry, whereas I felt just as definitely that teaching was my vocation.

Some measure of the influence of the small church is indicated in the lives of these young men. Great importance is frequently attached to the power of preaching, but in this place the greatest influence was exercised by dedicated persons rather than by preaching. The influence here at a crucial time in the lives of four of us was the young minister fresh from a Bristol College.

Another might be held responsible for my entry upon 'public speaking'. At fifteen I was still attending Sunday School. One morning after he had been speaking about the scripture story they had read, the old Superintendent suddenly called on me to say something. I was astounded. I had had no warning. But I had been brought up to do as I was asked, and I faced the small audience who could either 'like it or lump it'. If it was the latter, I would soon get to know all about it.

I realized that if I was to be effective I must deal with the story from a fresh angle, and in seconds I was thinking fast. What the story was I do not remember, but the children listened.

That was the start, and each Sunday I followed him. The principle I have tried to adhere to has been the same, an original approach.

History was also made when a football team was formed, with the minister as a playing member. Friendly fixtures were arranged, making possible a suitable choice of opponents. The presence of the minister caused interest, and more than once the warning was heard as our opponents took the field, "Mind, no swearing. Parson's playing." It was all greatly enjoyable. Travel was in a horse-drawn brake, slow but sure, cold and draughty sometimes, but the journey passed pleasantly in song and jest, good, old-fashioned banter, and in re-living, with some exaggeration, the exciting moments in the match.

Friendly on the field and friendly afterwards. A practice was established of taking members of the visiting team home for tea. After a hard game, often in rain, occasionally in snow or squelching mud, we sat in a homely kitchen, a huge fire blazing in the grate, round a table heaped as by a miracle with apple pies, mince pies, sandwiches and cakes, drinking countless cups of tea, strong, very strong tea, and eating till the jester called "Time!" It was a glorious way to end man's sixth day of labour.

Next day would be the happier for that. And in the pulpit would stand the man who could also use his head and his heart on the football field. We were proud of him.

(In the post-war period the church, like the nation, sought to recover from the weariness that had seized it. Then was born the idea to form a tennis club. Picnic teas began to take place, and it was not surprising that romances followed, and weddings too. And the Secretary proposed to the Treasurer, who thus became my wife.)

C3ED

BOYS WILL BE BOYS

There were four of us in the "gang", growing up together until the War separated us. Our parents attended chapel and we had to go there with them, but for Sunday School we were free from their supervision. John used to call for me and we varied the route to chapel according to inclination.

The less attractive road appealed to us far more. Made by the Council for pedestrians only, with previously used flagstones, badly laid, making walking an exercise in alertness, It was separated from the railway embankment by a fence of upright disused railway sleepers. The agile found it just as safe to walk along the top of the sleepers — irregular in height though they were — as to make one's way over the uneven flagstones ... and more exciting. But before you reached the fence or the uneven path, there was 'Chuckie's'.

'Chuckie's' was a place we were constantly warned against. A disused clay-hole with a steep fall like a cliff-face nearly all round, over the years it had become a miniature lake. At one point there was a very small beach, remnant of the track used long ago by carts entering and leaving the pit, where you could move safely if gingerly. A few feet out from the water's edge, however, you could be lost before help could be brought.

Despite the hazards it remained an attraction for young anglers with glass jar and simple line. In the summer the intrepid paddled there. As a diversion they chose thin, flat, smooth stones to throw, skimming the surface at such an angle that they would bounce regularly at lessening intervals across the smooth water till they sank. The pond was too wide for any throw to reach the far side, but they kept trying. In winter they stood on its frozen surface to see if it was strong enough for skating.

One Sunday, in the midst of such excitement, we suddenly remembered where we were supposed to be going and, with no watch, we were shocked to learn from a passer-by: "It's five to two."

We turned and ran. Already grubby, we ran for nearly another ten minutes, with dirty fingers pushing down a tightening collar, reaching Sunday School, even more begrimed, just as the first hymn was being sung — "Shall we gather at the river?" That was a cruel greeting.

Norman had kept a place for me beside him in spite of the crush, and turning with a knowing glint in his eye, he sang, "Shall we gather down at Chuckie's?" Then he whispered anxiously —"Look at your feet".

My boots were filthy! What would the grown-ups say when they saw me? I knew the answer to that one only too well, and it wasn't long in coming — as soon as we got into class, in fact. "Where on earth have you been, to get into that state?" said the teacher as soon as he saw me. "You'll be in trouble when you get home."

After that John and I had to keep to the more respectable route.

It was a pity, because the forbidden way had another powerful attraction in the slagheap. This was the local mountain, really a series of ranges on the edge of the village, stretching far into the fields as through the years the blast furnaces continued to disgorge waste, which was loaded onto flat bogeys and drawn by an ancient engine that defied gravity as it ground its way to the summit with groans that suggested it might disintegrate at any time. At the top it moved slowly and carefully along its elevated platform, pushing one bogey at a time until the bogey tilted at the end of the rails and the huge ball of slag slid of and came bounding down the slope.

Excitement rarely paled there. Sometimes on first impact with the solid heap the ball broke into a hundred red-hot fragments that shot in all directions to give a daylight fireworks display. Sometimes, when the ball had had longer to cool, it bounded down the slope without hitting anything and came slowly and harmlessly to rest. Occasionally the rolling mass struck a solid group of balls stuck near the top, forming an appreciable mound. If its momentum was sufficient, it bounded into the air to smash on the plain below. Every ball took a different path, met a different fate. But a fate to avoid was to get too close to the flying fragments or too near to those which still crackled threateningly through the hot crust, which had so far failed to disintegrate.

When no new tipping was in sight it was a simple matter to devise our own "follow the leader" among miniature peaks and craters. To scramble from one to the other, uneven and often slippery, and jump across water-filled craters marked our clothes, stockings and boots with the dust of the powdering rock. Before entering Sunday School, restoration efforts were applied as we hid round a corner. Wetting our hands, we rubbed the appropriate places on suit or boots, hoping to restore them to their "proper" state.

The introductory service over, the school dispersed to the small rooms or to places in the main hall where the teachers awaited us for the lesson. Ours was a man who knew how to keep discipline, and we were obliged to listen and then answer the questions he posed after his talk. He used to follow this up with a prayer, mentioning each of us by name. Very earnest and sincere, he really had our welfare at heart, and it is those qualities of his that I remember best. He never knew, though, the fun we had after Sunday School, when we went for a walk in the woods and sniggered at things he had said. We were not wicked really, just high-spirited boys who could not resist a little fun at the expense of a very serious-minded man, no matter how well—intentioned he was.

* * * * *

On one afternoon we went straight to the woods and to a field beyond, where Jack knew there was a peewit's nest. It was one of the largest fields in the district and how Jack found the nest surprised us. To cross to the nest, lying in the heart of this wide expanse of grass, made us easily visible from every side. It was John's turn for the egg. Quickly we left the spot and returned as casually as possible to the path, careful not to jostle John with the egg snug in his pocket.

We had nearly reached the stile that led into a small copse where we could pick up the track home, when - with split-second timing that was incredible - Police Constable Bowley appeared to confront us. ("Roly—Bowley" we called him, out of his hearing; everyone, though, called him stupid.) His huge bulk blocked the stile. He eased the strap of his helmet under the chin, adjusted it to its correct position, and smoothed his moustache. Leaning forward he rested one hand on each post and looked at us. Then he spoke, in a voice from a bottomless pit, a hint of menace in its depths. "Where have you lads been?"

To Sunday School, we told him — but that didn't satisfy him. He wanted to know what we were doing here, so far from the chapel, and we told him we were out for a walk. He also wanted to know where we lived. Luckily we were heading in the right direction for my house, so he seemed satisfied with that, to our relief.

"Well, see that you go straight home and don't let's have any more trespassing across the fields — or there'll be trouble."

As we stepped briskly to safe distance we heard his voice, suddenly quite gentle: "And just you lads keep away from birds' nests."

A few yards further on, from the side of Jack's mouth came a quiet plea of concern, "And just you lads keep away from John's pocket."

We were not bad, really. We were doing what boys have always done and always will do, and none the worse for it.

* * * * *

As we got older, our common interest in the church kept us together, though my meetings with the rest were limited to weekends. Then, as frequently happens, interests gradually diverged. Norman took seriously to woodcarving and cabinet-making, for which he had special ability. Jack started courting seriously.

John had left school and now helped in the family business as a travelling salesman, taking a pony and cart laden with fruit and vegetables to sell in the nearby villages. In the school holidays he would ask me to go with him for company. The days were long, and we travelled slowly. When we came to a steep hill, we jumped down and pushed at the rear to help the horse.

It was hard-earned money, especially in the winter—time, when potatoes, turnips, carrots and most vegetables (in their natural unwashed state) were ice—cold to the touch. We even handled apples, oranges and bananas that could easily have been described as frozen. John wore mittens to keep the hands, at least, warm, though the fingers were cut away for easy handling of the goods. But between houses we blew hard into our clenched fists and chafed our fingers for warmth. With the last call over we suddenly became light of heart and sang the horse into a gentle homeward trot along the dark lonely roads.

Boxes, bags and baskets had then to be carried into the store room, first for John's mother to see how much had been brought back and secondly for filling up again in readiness for the morrow. John handed over the money-bag and with amazing speed she counted it out. She had a good idea how much should be brought in, and, if it was disappointing, her rasping tongue rebuked us for having given too much credit. It was not, I thought, a good thing to work for your own mother, and after a few years of it, John thought so too. The wisdom of his choice was questionable. He went down the mines.

* * * * *

One of the special pleasures we shared was our adventures in reading. There was not a great deal of literature suitable for teenagers then, nor were there any public library facilities; moreover, we had little money to spend, so we shared what we bought.

Norman had most money and he specialized in Sexton Blake and Sherlock Holmes. It was thrilling to follow the exploits of these two very different detectives. My own purchase was the Boy's Own Paper, a serious attempt to satisfy intelligent interest — but the others found it rather heavy going. Jack and John bought lurid Westerns, and when we met on Saturday night there was general exchange.

Quite a remarkable development in publishing at this time caught my attention. It was the issue of a series of stories entitled "Books for the Bairns", produced under the editorship of W.T.Stead, selling at a penny each. Printed on rather thin paper of poor quality, with type that could be read only with good eyesight, and with a cover of thin, orange-coloured paper that tore easily, they were nonetheless amazing value. At this time, too, the works of Henty, Strang and Jules Verne were stirring our imagination, rousing in us the desire for adventure across the seas, under the seas and even on the moon. This sounds quite trivial today when science has accomplished feats which for us could exist only in the imagination, but our excitement in following Phileas Fogg round the world in eighty days, Henty in wars abroad, and Sexton Blake and Doctor Watson in dark mysteries stimulated our conversation every time we met. This was our Literature Class, which we organised ourselves.

Stead's issue of "The Penny Poets" was another landmark in the acquisition of a personal library. The same thin paper, which yellowed or browned with time, the same poor type, but each slim volume contained a collection of poems from great poets like Keats, Byron and Shelley plus others less well known. The later appearance of bound volumes of four of the poets was great encouragement to avid readers and writers.

It was such material costing only coppers that became treasure for many years. Additions came in the form of prizes from newspaper competitions — small volumes of typical Victorian tales with a moral, such as "Chris's Old Violin", and "How a Farthing made a Fortune."

It was no longer a case of wondering in vain who Dan with his can and his pan was, but an opening of windows onto the world outside (real or make-believe), stimulating the imagination and strengthening the desire to break out of that now seemingly drab sphere inhabited by four really quite ordinary village lads.

CR80

NIGHT OUT

"See you Saturday night in the Street."

That was clear enough. It was never misunderstood. One had only to be there, in the Street, the High Street, and one could not be missed. Somewhere between the Bridge and the Rex, Jack would meet John and Jonathan would meet Sally or someone else of the same sex who also would like to meet a boy, and who maybe was meeting some other girl equally disposed to meeting someone of the opposite sex. The possibilities were numerous. Saturday night was the night of the Prom. At the Bridge end the road narrowed, creating a bottleneck which tended to stem the easy flow of strollers, most of whom turned about and re-traced their steps to the other end, while courting couples, with the lanes and the woods in mind, passed beyond the Bridge to the open spaces.

At the east end of the Street where activity was less intense and the road wider, the attention turned to an ugly wooden hall, previously a garage which housed the newly-acquired petrol-engined road buses, but films, the exciting diversion for the multitudes, offered a chance for quicker financial returns than buses, so the wooden hut was converted into a cinema, not unlike the wooden structures of a new town in the Western States. The Rex, it was called, though such an association with kings could never occur to a mind free from mercenary motives.

The dim lights above the lurid posters enabled one to see better who were passing by and who were looking for others. It became a terminus, and there boy met girl and new roads were taken.

Saturday night was Everyman's night out. Working days were long, leisure evenings were short, and the walk, measured in miles there and back, from the surrounding villages made a visit to the town scarcely worthwhile. Saturday gave a longer spell, even for men working till mid-day, and to escape to the town was the great adventure of the week. The men knew which pubs had the best beer and the best company. Sometimes one of the company burst into song, with another improvising at the piano, and in such spontaneous fashion the entertainment of the evening proceeded. Few women went inside, except into a special room. The average pub was not considered a place for 'ladies'!

Before entering on the last stage of the evening out, the chaps stood about the street, taking in the scene and looking out for pals from other places to join them in a friendly drink or in more noisy revelry. Whatever happened in that evening would make their talk at the coalface on Monday morning and they would live the lively hours again – if they could remember it all. But at work they would be – they could not afford to miss a shift. And if they were puzzled to find a copy of The War Cry in their pockets, one of their pals would tell how, in a mood of exceeding generosity, he had given half-a-crown to a Salvation Army officer who wished them God's blessing and hoped they would get home safely.

For shopkeepers Saturday night was the night that ensured their living. Grocers, butchers, drapers, confectioners, shops large and small, stayed open till endless eleven of the clock, one hour short of Sunday. Some of them had been open from eight o'clock in the morning and girl assistants were exhausted and leg-weary from the long day. In the sudden flood that erupted on to the street with closing time the girls found escorts advisable.

Those who had left their unlighted village streets found the lights of the town exciting in contrast. The main street itself was ordinarily only faintly lit by fish-tail gas burners enclosed in a lantern surmounting the lamp-post, so faintly lit that one might describe the light as but rendering darkness visible. It was from the shop windows and from the market stalls that light emerged to throw a vaporous canopy of silver-brown over the whole length of the street at little more than roof height. Those not actually using the footpaths on their shopping hunt walked the road itself, the gentle light revealing the irregular lines and shuffling groups of less purposeful wanderers who moved back and forth in ambling leisure to see all that might be seen in their abandon to the dim pleasures of the evening in the Street.

Many of the shops were badly lighted, fishtail burners on brackets of four failing to dispel the gloom. Several had adopted the novel incandescent gas mantle emitting its white searchlight from a brittle mantle, beautiful while it lasted, but duration uncertain, especially in swishing draught. Greatest enterprise was in those shops where electric power had been newly installed, though the clear-glass bulbs with yellowish filaments, rather cheerless, were but a promise of brighter things to come. The fiercest, most compelling lights were those which illuminated the stalls lining both sides of the street, paraffin lamps with the naked flame of swinging burners hung over the contents of the stall and hissing angrily, or those with incandescent burners fitted to pressured lamps, the bright, silent illumination giving a new class distinction in the row of travelling salesmen. On a windy night when the canvas covers of the stalls flapped noisily and wildly, and the burning lamps swung through a wide arc, one wondered for the safety of the stall-keeper as he dodged below the hissing tongues thrusting to and fro, visible above the shoulders of a thick coat, hid in turn beneath a white coat, the mark of clean intent in the purveyance of fresh-boiled sweets, creamy toffee and caramels, broken biscuits and broken chocolate, jelly jujubes, cough candy and candy rock. On the other side of the screen his wife, white-bedecked too, declaring the delicious quality of tripe and onions, jellied eels, calf's feet, pig's cheek, chitterlings and black pudding. Here was no novelty, but everything that had stood the test of time, and unwittingly, though the women intuitively knew these were a good buy, anticipating the decisions of the new race of dieticians with the advantage of their science to tell folk what and when to buy.

Next in line were the stalls which smelt of the earth, with potatoes, cabbages and cauliflowers, carrots, turnips, peas and beans in season, oranges and apples set out in red and golden pyramids, and date, the singular specially used to describe the solid block of dates, two feet by one by one, pressed so hard that hammer and chisel were often required to break off a portion. A penn'orth of date was a luxury long in eating, and long remembered.

Travelling salesmen shouted their produce with glee as they faced across the footpath the regular shopkeepers resentful of their stand. All along the line they stretched, salesmen for the day. There were pies and peas that you ate standing by the stall, and scores of things needed for the home every day - bootlaces and blacking, brushes, pins and needles, soap and candles, towels and dusters; there were few novelties. Life was simple and purses were shallow, but there was more choice on the stalls, and one took a gamble. For a very special treat there were ornaments for household decoration. Worcester, Derby and Doulton were not names to look for here, but wherever these things had been baked, their crude crimsons and bronzes, greens and ochres sent a shiver through the bowels. The loud champions of this coloured clay drew a crowd that returned home with arms fondling news-wrapped troubadours, angel faces, sitting dogs and descending doves that would find a place on window ledge, mantelpiece or cupboard top till a new generation gave it to a jumble sale.

For sheer entertainment, and this was important in days when the cinema had scarce arrived and no variety show came near but once a year, the knowing ones moved to that part of the street where there was no background of shops, but a church hall at a greater depth from the road than the shops. Here the select band of invaders chose their pitch, a line of small lorries or flat carts hired for the occasion from a local lad having his night out, or a space delineated by orange-boxes bought from stall-holders within which were piled the goods about to be offered at great sacrifice, without reserve and with only one thing in mind, the satisfaction of the customer. In this area experience and skilled salesmanship were at a premium. Cheap jokes, funny stories and unbridled oratory made listening great fun and buying often expensive... but, of course, one must pay for one's entertainment, one could not have it all ways.

At Number One stand a white streamer proclaimed in striking red: THE GREATEST LIVING AUTHORITY ON HERBS, PILLS, POTIONS.

The fellow so acclaimed was a portly figure, six feet in height, hair and tongue so smooth that few would dream of confuting. For him no doctor's prescription could match, no mixture of brown or white could equal the plants and the potions whose healing powers he had wrestled from the earth. He held his audience spellbound. They compared him with the parson and the preachers they would hear next day and the Member of Parliament who was coming next week. This man had everything, golden voice, rhythmic tongue, unfailing word, and best of all, he knew their life, he knew their ailments, they felt him suffering with them as he spoke. From Mother Earth, he said, came the gifts of God to nourish and strengthen the children of God. In the plants of the hedgerow, the grasses of moor and meadow, the berries of tree and flower, the roots of rare plants from abroad, Mexico, the Indies and far Cathay, from all these came the gifts of nature to make up the deficiencies which our ignorant ways of living had caused. He, through his special study of the subject, in lands beyond the seas as well as in remote corners of this little island, had learned the secrets of replenishment, which he now wished to pass on to his fellows through his packets, his pills and his potions.

Was it rheumatism that distressed them? Arthritis? Or simple stomach ache, disordered liver, cramp, weak heart, breathlessness, lassitude —

any ailment, except downright laziness — these all could be cured by these amazing compounds, which he brought to them at ridiculous prices. A packet of herbs, a box of herbal pills, a bottle of herbal brew — everything the same price, one shilling.

"It's worth the money just to listen," they said. And they bought the pills and herbs and brew as if to escape impending doom. They swore by him, this wizard of herbs and oratory.

At Number Two stand was a new rival. Folk crowded round, even blocking the road to a rumbling cart whose horse threatened to close the market when the packed crowd surged against him. Police directed them to the church hall side of the stand, and horse and cart passed on to the end of their busy day.

Here was sensation at its highest! The reason? On the rostrum stood a black man, big enough and smart enough to be a gentleman prizefighter. He had taken off his coat, showing his white shirt with cuffs neatly turned back, gold rings on several fingers of each hand, a heavy gold chain slung across his waistcoat from pocket to pocket, teeth white as pearls, eyes shining from the dark face. A rare physical specimen and a rare occupation too. A travelling dentist!

Without any College training, he boasted, without any instruments, but by the exercise of the most remarkable gift of manipulation, he offered his services for the extraction of teeth by the use of his fingers alone, from the smallest of dainty mouths or the largest and strongest jaws, he never failed. Painlessly and with bleeding that was negligible he would remove the offending tooth, and all for half-a-crown, to cover the cost of the most soothing, cleansing mouthwash that would make extraction a memory, proof against all infection, warding off all other oral trouble, toothache, gumboils, ulcers or any other affliction of that part of the anatomy.

And they believed him. It was thrilling to hear, exciting to watch. There was no lack of folk who would trust themselves to the fingers of this traveller, and when the queue for extractions was over, they formed a queue for the gargle at a shilling a time. Incredibly he sold out quickly. He vanished quickly too, and never returned.

After so much excitement among the crowds and a few chats with questing girls, it was time for refreshment, and for another rite in the evening's ceremonies - eating fried chips, gloriously golden-brown chips. No night out was complete without a penn'orth of chips.

Interspersed among the stalls throughout the street were the vans, so conspicuous by their number and their colour that they earned the town a reputation for chips. "You smell them a mile away." They were built in caravan style, painted gaudy yellow and red, a chimney protruding through the roof, and a bright glare on the ground below from the coke fire enclosed in a well slung between front and rear wheels. In the well stood the salesman-fryer, facing pans of boiling fat suspended over a coke furnace. At knee level he fed the fiery furnace, whose heat warmed the faces and the anticipations of the customers pressing round the van. At waist level his hands held the wire-griddled pans half-filled with fresh-cut chips, shaking them gently but briskly to keep them browning and cooking through. When his eye discerned they were done, he lifted the grid, shook it to drain off the fat and poured the steaming, sumptuous load into a warm empty dish. Then, the boiling pan replenished, he proceeded to serve. With a sheet of newspaper as base, resting it in the left hand, he smartly depressed it over his palm by a deft touch of the right hand, placed a small piece of grease-proof paper in the centre, and onto this concave, improvised plate the chips were ladled, one spoonful, two, three, for your penny or twopence. A child might even ask for a ha'porth.

From the huge canister of salt one sprinkled according to taste, and finally from a dark brown bottle with a dark brown cork, pierced to let the vinegar pass, one splashed the vinegar to heart's content.

And there, in the street, or withdrawn just round the corner, whether folk watched or not, one stood, finger and thumb making swift despatch as long ago primitive man handled his food, till all that was left in the sunken centre was the vinegar with tiny fragments of brown chip floating upon it. One raised the paper carefully for this last stage, threw back the head, opened the mouth, and in one second the miniature lake streamed down the throat. The cry that followed was of simple, ecstatic satisfaction. Then the crumpled, greasy paper was thrown to the ground.

A penn'orth of chips was a rite that had faithfully to be performed. Standing round the corner, half-a-dozen together, chips in hand, quipping with the heartiness the smoking meal evoked, they were together, a community of their own, sharing this common meal. Grown men might show the same heartiness in company over a pint, but they had not reached that stage, yet they were just as much together. When reluctance to be seen indulging first showed itself, it was a sign of a new consciousness, a new modesty, new social difference. Pals separated, the gang disintegrated. But to their dying day many never gave it up. For them nothing compared with the smell of the vans in the distance, their cosy warmth, and the golden chips freshly hot and sizzling to appease youthful hunger.

It was as a boy that I made my trips to the town on Saturday night and always with father. Mother used to stay at home with the young family. Father was given instructions for shopping, I accompanied him and with the net bag in my charge I returned when shopping was completed and safely delivered to mother the fresh fish, cod usually, sausage and pork pies that were a great speciality. The fish and the sausage were cooked that evening to be eaten cold for breakfast on Sunday morning.

As I grew older the journey developed a closer relation between father and son that only the nature of the terrain made possible. Away from the house we moved across the road into the dark, down an uneven path between gardens unevenly fenced, a path in places deeply runnelled by heavy rains and calling for careful step. Then we crossed the Green, choosing the hard ridges to walk on, lit up for a few moments by the sudden glare of the blast furnaces. From momentary glare to sudden darkness made the darkness yet deeper and we stumbled against each other, or against the fence, into a rut deeper than usual, and we learned to save each other from falling. Then on a smoother part of the way, when he knew the walls were broken down, he would say something he had on his mind. Someone had been telling him that I had been seen talking and walking with a girl. His informant said she wasn't any good and that I should be warned. So, "Be careful what you do," he said. I did not know what he meant and he did not expand. I was not worried about the advice. I was more interested in who might have my welfare so much at heart and how many daughters she might have.

It was when crossing the Green on another occasion that I took the chance to talk about the future. I was nearly eighteen, my time at the Grammar School was nearing its close, and my thoughts were of College... a London college. No other place had entered my mind. The fees? I could not summon courage to mention the amount. With the family at home and our limited resources, I felt I dare not ask for such special consideration for myself. And yet I wanted to go. So, in the dark, when smooth going was assured, I broached the subject, describing the excitement among the lads at school as they sent away their applications, nearly all to local colleges.

To my astonishment father asked, "Where do you wish to apply?" though I think he knew. I told him. A quiet hum followed. Then the next question. "How much is it there?" I told him. The hum was broken by a nervous cough, and then I felt the still air.

"Then there will be train fare to London each term," he said, "and other things. It's a lot of money for us to find."

"Yes", I agreed, scarce daring even to say that. There was no grant to help either.

"But we'll do it," he said. "Ma and I have talked about it. We want you to go."

I could have screamed for joy, and at the same time was reduced to silence, no more than to say, "Thanks, I hope it will be all right."

In the dark, across the Green broken words and a deep humility in both of us, I could sense it. The decision was confirmed that opened out a new life for me.

We stumbled through the darkness over the track lighted only from the soft reflection of furnace glow from a ceiling of grey cloud, and emerged on the dim gas-lit road to the town. The bell in the church tower hung silent against the night. I could have pealed it for joy.

It was almost the last time I went across the Green.

C3EOCEEO